First Card Making

First Card Making

Simple projects for card makers

Paula Pascual

COLLINS & BROWN

Contents

Workshop
20

Baby Shower
58

Birth Announcement
60

Children's Party
64

Pretty in Pink
68

18th Birthday Party
70

21st Birthday
72

Girls-Only Party
74

Man's Birthday Card
76

Graduation
78

Engagement
Announcement
82

Engagement Party
84

First published in the United Kingdom in 2011 by
Collins & Brown
10 Southcombe Street
London
W14 0RA

An imprint of Anova Books Company Ltd

Copyright © Collins & Brown 2011
Text and project copyright © Paula Pascual 2011

This book was originally published as Creative Card Making in 2005

Photography by Colin Bowling, Michael Wicks and Sian Irvine

A CIP catalogue for this book is available from the British Library.

ISBN 978-1-84340-614-3

10 9 8 7 6 5 4 3 2 1

Reproduction by Mission Productions, Hong Kong
Printed and bound by 1010 Printing International Ltd, China

This book can be ordered direct from the publisher at
www.anovabooks.com

Introduction

I have been making cards for many years, not only for myself but also for other people. Often I am asked to do invitations to weddings or other special events and although this is very similar to making just one birthday card it is not quite the same. When making large batches of cards, the most important aspect to consider is that you will need to make many cards that are all the same – or, at the very least, that have the same design.

Sometimes, making lots of cards takes far more time than you expect and some techniques take longer than others, but all the cards in this book have been specially designed so large quantities can be made quickly. I have also included a useful chart (see pages 14–15) that will help you determine what project to try and what products to use. And remember: the best way to make lots of cards in a short time is to set up a mini production line, so you do all the cutting first, then all the scoring, then the sticking.

Gift giving is also a part of weddings and parties. How many times do you have a present to give but don't have wrapping paper that's just right? I'll show you not only how to make cards, but also how to make simple boxes, bags and tags, decorate wrapping paper and how to wrap a present beautifully with just pieces of scrap paper. Using these basic techniques as a guide, you can make boxes and paper to match your card and have a fully co-ordinated event!

There are so many different techniques to master and many wonderful ways to add designs and colours: scoring, folding and cutting, decorating edges, sticking and fixing, creative uses of glue, stamping, making apertures, stencil embossing, creating polymer clay embellishments, and making inserts. These are great skills to learn, and will enable you to design your own cards, giving that really special personal touch. I do hope you enjoy making the projects in this book as much as I have enjoyed working on it.

Paula Pascual

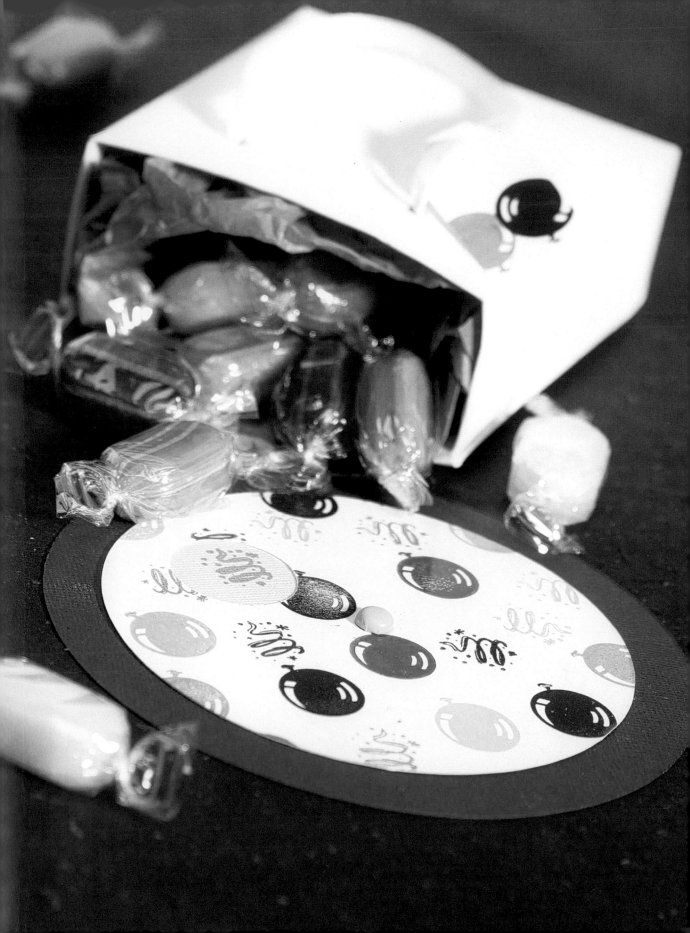

How to use this book

There are many elements to consider when making cards, but there is nothing quite so satisfying for a crafter than to see a beautiful card finished and ready to be mailed! Handmade cards, invitations and gift wraps mean far more to the recipient, because you have put time and energy into making something special. You can also add extra details, personal touches and make them far more beautiful than a shop-bought version.

The projects in this book are graded from those that are quick to make, to those that take time and require more skill. They are all explained in simple language and are designed to introduce just a few new techniques at a time, building up confidence steadily and surely.

A comprehensive workshop section at the beginning of the book illustrates the basics, so you can see exactly what to do. Easy-to-follow text will teach you all the techniques you need to create the projects in the book. Each technique has a reference number, which is used for cross-referencing in the patterns.

The project section features 27 stylish cards for every occasion. Each one is accompanied by clear text and step-by-step photographs showing the key stages for easy reference as you work. The instructions for each project contain reference numbers, which direct you to the relevant technique in the Workshop, should you need to learn a new technique or be reminded of a familiar one.

PROJECTS

QUICK CARD	MEDIUM DIFFICULTY	NEEDS TIME
Baby Shower	Pretty in Pink	Birth Announcement
Girls-Only party	18th Birthday Party	Children's Party
Man's Birthday card	21st Birthday	Wedding Folder
With Love	Engagement Announcement	New Home
Graduation	Engagement Party	Red Valentine
White Wedding	At Home	Easter Eggs
25th Anniversary	Retirement	Christmas Trees
50th Anniversary	Thanksgiving	
Fourth of July	Christmas Presents	
Halloween	Glittery Snowflakes	

Tools

* A small rubber-tipped hammer
* Eyelet setter and hole punch
* Anywhere punches in different shapes
* Setting mat or old cutting mat
* Shaped punches
* Hand punch
* Paper trimmer (not shown)
* Paper guillotine
* Paper piercer
* Tweezers
* Stylus or embossing tool
* Brass stencils
* Soft eraser
* Makeup applicators
* Water brush
* Soft, broad and fine-tip paintbrushes
* Emery board
* Scoring board
* Bone folder
* Scuffers or sanding blocks
* Scissors
* Metal-edged ruler
* Craft knife or X-acto knife
* Pencil
* Small, sharp scissors
* Circle cutter
* Spray bottle
* Rubber stamps
* Self-healing cutting mat
* Applicator or stir sticks
* Darning needle
* Orange stick
* Clip pen
* Rolling pin

Materials

* Paper and card
* Ribbon and fibres (such as raffix, string, thread and yarn)
* Low-tack tape
* Vellum tape
* Double-sided tape
* Sticky-dots tape
* Black and coloured ink pads
* Imitation gold leaf
* Brads, eyelets and buttons
* Self-adhesive foam dots and pads
* Paper flowers and other embellishments
* Watercolour brush paints or markers
* PVA glue
* Embossing powder
* Glitter
* Spray adhesive
* Silicone glue
* Double-sided adhesive sheet
* 3-D glue
* Rubber-stamp cleaner
* Heat gun
* Paper clips
* Spray fixative or hair spray
* Craft chalks
* Silicone compound
* Polymer clay
* Gold and silver-leafing pen
* Fine wire
* Beads
* Cotton balls
* Embroidery floss

Work sheet

Questions you need to ask yourself to help you choose the right project.

What is the event or occasion?

_____

_____

Who are the cards being made for?

_____

_____

Which colour scheme has been chosen?

_____

_____

How many are you making?

_____

_____

How long do you have to make them?

_____

_____

What size?

_____

_____

✶ Remember, if you are making items for somebody else you will need more time. It is likely they will want to see the design first. Do not order the materials until the project has been approved.

✶ If this is already chosen, make the cards in those colours.

✶ This is a very important question. You need to know not only how many working days you have (important if you need to order and receive materials through the mail), but also how many hours you can work on the project. The answer will allow you to choose the most suitable project – each one has an estimate of the time required to make it.

✶ For special events like weddings and christenings you may want to keep the card forever, therefore it is best to use acid-free products, which will last longer.

✶ Always make ten percent more, if possible. If you are making invitations, there is always a chance that more will be required than originally thought. Also, as these cards are handmade, sometimes some of them will not be as perfect as you might wish. After all, mistakes do happen! A few extra cards will avoid problems later.

✶ Standard-size envelopes are the most easily available, but that doesn't mean the cards have to be standard. The shape can be totally different as long as the cards fit inside perfectly. Check the postal rates for non-standard envelopes, as well.

Budget and shopping list

Are you worried that the invitations are going to cost more than ready-made ones? Or that you are going to forget to buy vital material? This budget and shopping list will help keep things under control.

Material	Description	Total	Material	Description	Total
* White card			* Watermark ink pad		
* Coloured card 1			* Black ink pad		
* Coloured card 2			* Coloured ink pad 1		
* Prescored card 3			* Coloured ink pad 2		
* Vellum card			* Colouring pencils		
* Patterned paper 1			* Leafing pen		
* Patterned paper 2			* Pigment powder		
* Envelope			* Paint		
* Insert			* Chalk		
* Double-sided tape			* Fixative		
* PVA glue			* Charms		
* Sticky foam			* Die cuts		
* Vellum tape			* Buttons		
* Silicone glue			* Feathers		
* Spray adhesive			* Tags		
* Dimensional glue			* Wire		
* Eyelets			* Crystals		
* Brads			* Embellishment		
* Ribbon 1			* Stickers		
* Ribbon 2			* Polymer clay 1		
* Fibres			* Polymer clay 2		
* Glitter			* Gold leaf		
* Sticky-dots tape			* Silver leaf		

Tools

* Paper trimmer	* Bone folder	* Sanding block	* Brass stencil 2
* Cutting mat	* Sharp scissors	* Rubber stamp 1	* Brass stencil 3
* Craft knife and blades	* Small, sharp scissors	* Rubber stamp 2	* Circle cutter
* Tweezers	* Soft brush	* Rubber stamp 3	* Paper piercer
* Pencil	* Medium brush	* Punch 1	* Eyelet setter
* Soft eraser	* Scoring template	* Punch 2	* Hole punch
* Metal-edged ruler	* Template 1	* Punch 3	* Rubber stamp cleaner
	* Template 2	* Brass stencil 1	* Water brush

Fonts and text layout for inserts

So now you have chosen the perfect design for the wedding or party invitation, the baby announcement or the birthday card, it's time to think about the text inside. It's all very well to have a beautiful design on the outside, but the text inside the card is just as important. Here are a few tips on how to create a co-ordinating interior layout that matches the outside.

Fonts

Today every computer comes supplied with a huge number of fonts, which can make the choice difficult. But, as always, the best rule is keep it simple. There are three basic styles of fonts: the serif, the sans serif and the graphic.

1 The serif types are the fonts that have a little adornment, or serif, at each termination of the letter (like the font that is used in this text). They are the fonts that are most commonly used in print because they are considered more legible. They are discreet, don't catch our attention as much as others, and they are timeless.

Together with their parents

JULIE EDWARDS AND KEVIN ASHBY

Request the pleasure of your company
at their marriage

Saturday 5th March 2011
Five o'clock in the evening

Brasted Manor House

A reception will follow after the ceremony

Checklist

There are several elements that need to be considered, although most of these are points that you will already have discussed before deciding on the design of the card. Ask yourself these questions:

1. What is the general style of the project?
It might be fancy and elaborate, simple and graphic or perhaps elegant and classical. This will influence the choice of font and the positioning or alignment of the text.

2. What is the colour scheme of the event?
The colour inside obviously needs to co-ordinate with the colours used on the outside.

3. What size is the card?
The text area for a long thin insert is different to that of a non-regular shape or a square one.

Julie Edwards and Kevin Ashby

Invite you to celebrate their marriage

Saturday 5th March 2011
Five o'clock in the evening

Brasted Manor House

A reception will follow after the ceremony

Mr. and Mrs. David Edwards

*request the honour of your presence at
the marriage of their daughter*

Julie Edwards

to

Mr. Kevin Ashby

Saturday 5th March 2011 at

five o'clock in the evening

Brasted Manor House

2 Sans-serif fonts don't have serifs, so they look simpler and less detailed than the serif fonts. They are great for a contemporary or understated look. They also combine beautifully with decorative fonts as shown below.

 3 Graphic fonts are subdivided into two groups – script fonts and display or decorative ones (see above). Many commercially produced wedding invitations use the script-type fonts, which give an elegant and classical look. The display types are experimental and illustrative, often best for children's cards. Both types are less legible than other fonts, so it is best to keep to as little text as possible when using them.

Combining fonts can be very effective (see left), but if you add too many – more than two different types – the layout may look messy. The best option is to play with the different sizes and styles of one font, like Garamond or Helvetica, and use the different weights that are available (for instance, light, regular, bold, black). My favourite combination is a sans-serif font for the main body text with a very ornamental script just for the names.

Using just capitals is perfect for an elegant, yet contemporary, feel. It works especially well with sans-serif fonts, but also looks good with serif ones. However, never use it with script fonts.

Alignment

Centring the text is a good option if there is only a brief amount, such as on an invitation. To add visual interest try to vary the length of the lines. Avoid justifying the text – making it run right from one edge to the other in one solid block – as this makes it difficult to read and often creates uneven white spaces between words and letters. Centring the lines of text is a classical option that will work with both a script font or a serif one, as in the far right example.

When it comes to aligning the text down one side, in general it is a safe bet to opt for the left hand side, especially for a large block of text. However, invitations don't have much text and traditionally are centred, so a left-aligned text will have a modern feel. It is therefore best combined with a sans-serif font, as in the example right. Aligning the text to the right is an unusual option that can be very effective if used with a modern type.

Also consider the shape of the insert (see pages 43–44 for details on how to make an insert). To check how the text layout will look, draw a box the size and shape of the insert to see how different fonts and alignments will look within the space available.

Together with their parents

Julie Edwards and Kevin Ashby

Request the pleasure of your
company at their marriage

Saturday 5th March 2011
Five o'clock in the evening

Brasted Manor House

A reception will follow after the
ceremony

Spaces inbetween letters

Most text programs offer a tracking device that will allow you to add more space in between letters within the same word. This will give a more relaxed and airy feel that is perfect for an understated look. It works very well with text all in capitals – as in the example on page 16 – but you must avoid it completely with script (Quark is shown here, but Word offers a similar function, called character spacing).

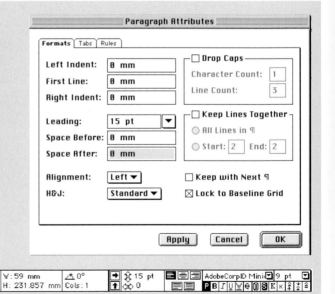

Adding colour

Although it seems that adding colour should be very easy, it is actually very difficult to print text in the exact same colour as the outside of a card. The best way is to print a section of text, in the font and size that you plan to use, in as many different colours as possible from the program's colour palette. The example below shows text in different shades of black, as these come by default even with a very basic text processor. Try out different variations with coloured text. If none of the standard colours is the one you want, then try any of the other colour options that most programs can provide. In this way you should be able to find a printed colour that is close to the colour scheme of the card.

Julie Edwards

Julie Edwards

Julie Edwards

Julie Edwards

Julie Edwards

Julie Edwards

Julie Edwards

Julie Edwards

Julie Edwards

Julie Edwards

Mr. and Mrs. David A. Edwards
request the honour of your presence
at the marriage of their daughter

Julie Edwards
to
Mr. Kevin Ashby

Saturday 5th March 2011
at five o'clock in the evening

Brasted Manor House

Adding Motifs

Sometimes a simple motif can make a huge difference in an insert. It can be a motif that you have designed, an ornament from a font or just a beautiful monogram. It can be printed with the rest of the text or just stamped. If you opt for the last option make sure that you have a template to follow, so the motif will be perfectly placed every time.

Workshop

Use this section to learn the basic techniques you need to create the projects in this book. You can use many of them on their own to create simple items, but the Projects section shows how to combine several techniques to give detailed and interesting results. Here you will also learn how to make different gift wraps and boxes and how to wrap presents.

   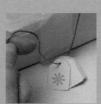 

▮1 Scoring

Scoring the fold lines, before you fold card or thick paper to make a card or box, gives you a much neater and more professional-looking finish. Experiment with different techniques on scrap card or paper.

With a bone folder

1 Take a card and find the centre with a ruler. Make a tiny mark with a pencil at the top and bottom.

2 With the point of a bone folder, score a line along a ruler held between the two marks. Place an old computer mouse mat underneath to make scoring easier.

Using a scoring board

1 Use the markings on the template to line up the card. Holding the card steady, run the point of the bone folder down the groove that matches your desired fold. This will create a scored line in the shape of a 'valley.'

Folding

1 Score the fold line and flatten the fold with the broad side of the bone folder. Most cards fold better if you have the 'valley' on the inside, but vellum folds much easier the other way around.

▮2 Cutting

Cutting can be done with a craft knife, guillotine or paper trimmer. Experiment with different cutting tools and scrap card or paper, holding the card or paper firmly while cutting, so the cut will be straight.

With a craft knife

1 Take a piece of card and make a tiny mark with a pencil at the top and bottom exactly where you want to cut. Make sure you have a self-healing cutting mat underneath.

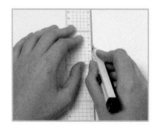

2 Draw the blade of a craft knife against a ruler, held between the two marks. When cutting with a craft knife always use a metal ruler.

With a guillotine or paper trimmer

1 Measure and mark as in Step 1 for the craft knife.

2 When cutting with a new trimmer or guillotine always try it out on a spare piece of the card you wish to cut, because different papers react in a different way.

3 Hold the paper firmly while cutting (it tends to slide and leave an angled cut), and bring the blade down. Cutting and storing your cards is a tedious and time consuming job. Consider buying pre-cut and ready-scored cards to save time, however this is a more expensive option.

3 | Tearing edges with water

This technique gives an attractive deckle edge.

1 Paint a line of water along the outer edge of a card with a fine-tip paintbrush, then repeat on the inner edge.

2 Gently tear downward, to remove a strip along the wet line.

4 | Colouring with inkpads

Ink pads are a clean and simple way of applying colour.

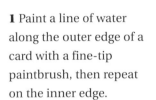 

1 Create a deckle edge, as shown above in Tearing edges with water.

2 Gently rub an ink pad down the torn edge.

5 | Colouring with pens

Use either a felt-tip or brush pen.

1 Run the end or side of a coloured felt-tipped pen along the edge of the paper. Try to move at an even speed using constant pressure.

6 | Colouring different edges

Using different colours adds interest.

1 Score and fold down the top right corner of the front of your card.

2 Colour the outside edge with one colour, and the inside edge with a contrasting colour.

3 Fasten a co-ordinating flower to the folded corner. The finished card is simple but eye-catching.

7 Edge punches

Some punches are specifically designed for edges.

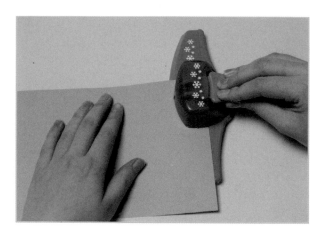

1 Line up the punch on the top half of a card so the edge of the card is straight against the edge of the punch. Punch out the pattern.

2 Aligning the punch with the pattern on the top half of the card, punch the bottom half (with large cards, you may have to punch several times to complete an edge).

8 Double-sided tape

This is a clean and quick method, which works best for attaching large pieces with straight edges.

1 Apply a strip of double-sided tape to the edges on the back of an item you want to stick.

2 Trim the tape to within the edges.

3 Peel off a short length of each backing tape and fold this 'tag' away at an angle.

4 Position the item onto a card, holding the exposed tape away from the surface as you move it around. When you are happy with the positioning, press the exposed tape down to hold the item in place.

5 Pull the tags away, smoothing down the item as you go.

9 Sticky-dots tape

This kind of tape is formed of tiny, double-sided sticky dots. Some tapes have applicators that make applying them easier. You can use it as you would use double-sided tape, only there's no backing to remove. And it's even better for sticking items that have irregular shapes.

1 Apply a strip of sticky dots to the opposite edges of a card or piece of paper that you want to stick.

2 Sticky-dots tape is also excellent for fastening flat ribbons, even rickrack, because the dots will only stick to where there is ribbon.

10 PVA adhesive

This is a useful glue for very small or non-porous items. PVA adhesive dries clear, but use only tiny amounts so it doesn't wrinkle the card or paper.

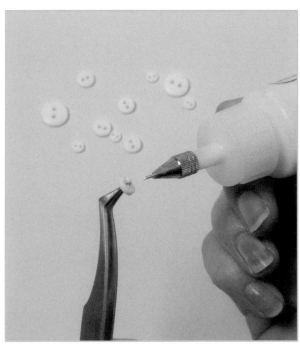

1 Hold small items with tweezers as you apply the adhesive.

2 Use the tweezers to apply the items to a card.

11 Spray adhesive

This is one of the best adhesives, but it is messy and quite expensive. Only use it to glue large surfaces, or with paper or material that is very delicate or intricate.

1 To protect your work area, put the paper face down inside a plastic tub or cardboard box. Shake the can and spray all over the back to get a thin, even coat.

2 Position the paper onto a backing, holding it with both hands and ensuring that there are no wrinkles.

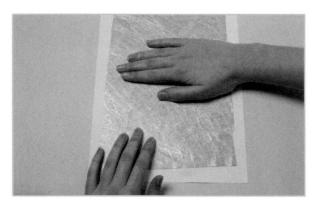

3 Use your hand to smooth it down and check that it is firmly stuck.

12 Self-Adhesive dots

A 3-D effect is always appealing, and foam dots make it easy.

1 Peel the adhesive dots off the sheet and apply to the back of an item.

2 Peel the backing off each dot and press the item onto a card.

13 Silicone glue

Although it's messy and smelly, silicone glue is an excellent adhesive for odd shaped embellishments and uneven, textured card and paper.

1 Use an applicator to take some silicone glue out of the tube.

2 Dab the glue onto an embellishment you wish to attach.

3 Press the embellishment onto a card.

14 Ribbon

Ribbon can be used to attach an item to a card and add decoration and texture. There are thousands of ribbons to choose from – there are no restrictions as to colour, design or width – and they can co-ordinate wrapping, cards and tags.

Using two holes

1 Decide where you want the two holes – in this case, 2.5cm (1in.) from each side edge – and make a mark with a pencil at each spot.

2 Punch the holes with a hole punch.

3 Push the ribbon from the back of the card through the left hole, and through the right hole to the back again, leaving a 'tail' of ribbon at each end.

4 Through the opposite hole, push each ribbon end back to the front.

27

15 Attaching thin ribbon

PVA glue is the best way to glue thin ribbon (see PVA adhesive, page 25).

1 Make a mark with a pencil where you want the ribbon.

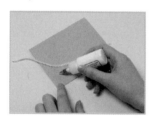

2 Dab PVA onto each mark (you can also apply the PVA directly onto the ribbon, then fasten it to the card).

3 Position the ribbon and press down firmly.

16 Organza and transparent ribbon

These are lovely but difficult to glue. Vellum tape is perfect because it disappears under the ribbon.

1 Apply the vellum tape to a card and cut off the excess.

2 With a bone folder, burnish down the tape.

3 Peel off the backing.

4 Position the ribbon and press down gently to adhere it to the tape.

5 Turn the card over and cut off the excess ribbon. It is much easier to cut a perfect edge in line with the card if you cut from the back, as you can see the edge of the card.

17 Attaching non-porous objects

Found objects like candles and sparklers are fun decorations, but it can be a challenge to stick them on.

Piercing holes

This technique does not require any glue at all, but it will only work for items that are long and very thin.

1 Position the items where you want them on the card, then make two marks with a pencil where each item will 'stitch' in and out. With a craft knife make small cuts where the marks are.

2 Push the tip of each item in and out through the cuts. Sometimes you may need to make the cuts a little bit bigger, to push the item through.

Using all-purpose adhesive

Normally it's best not to use this glue, since it is very wet and tends to wrinkle the paper, but it is the best way to attach big or heavy non-porous items.

1 Position the items to be glued on a card. One by one, lift up each item and apply a small amount of glue to the card, then replace the item gently so the glue doesn't squeeze out.

Attaching fibres to a tag

1 Fold the fibres in half, forming a loop, and push the loop through a tag.

2 Thread the ends through the loop and gently pull.

18 Attaching with eyelets

Eyelets are a great way to attach any flat item or pieces of vellum. There are three standard sizes for eyelets: 1.5mm (¹⁄₁₆in.), 3mm (¹⁄₈in.) – which is the most common – and 5mm (³⁄₁₆in.). For each size you will need a different hole punch and setter.

1 To make sure the eyelet is in the perfect place, cut both the card and paper to the right size and position the paper on top of the card on a cutting mat, then make a hole with the anywhere punch, using a hammer.

2 Lift the hole punch carefully to check that both paper and card have been perforated.
If not, replace the punch and hammer it again.

3 Holding the card and paper together, place the eyelet in the hole.

4 Turn the card over so the back of the eyelet is showing.

5 Using an eyelet setter, set the eyelet, using the hammer.

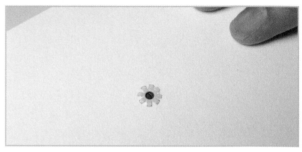

6 Different setters finish the eyelet in a different way, so if the back of the eyelet is going to be exposed you may need to consider this when purchasing the set – some will leave a rough, scratchy or unattractive surface.

19 Attaching with brads

Brads are similar to eyelets but they don't need a special tool to fasten them in place. Although most brads have a round head, there are many different sizes, shapes and colours, such as squares, rectangles, keys and snowflakes available. A nice insert is always useful for covering up a mark left by a brad.

1 To make sure the brad is in the perfect place, cut both the card and paper to the right size and position the paper on top of the card on a cutting mat, then make a hole with the anywhere hole punch, using a hammer.

2 When working with different shapes or sizes, such as these circular cards, you will need to centre each layer separately.

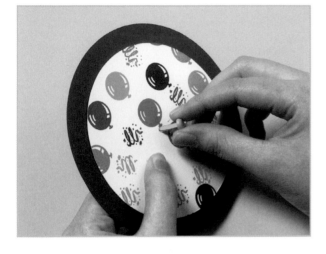

3 Holding the card and paper together, place the brad in the hole.

4 Turn the card over, then flatten the ends of the brad.

20 Double-sided adhesive sheet and gold leaf

Real gold leaf is wonderful but expensive. Luckily, imitation gold leaf gives cards almost exactly the same look for a fraction of the cost. It is messy, but used with a double-sided adhesive sheet, it is an easy way of adding small, rich gold backgrounds. Every piece of gold leaf, no matter how small, can be used to fill gaps, so keep all of your scraps.

1 Peel off the backing on one side of an adhesive sheet.

2 Apply a piece of imitation gold leaf onto the exposed adhesive.

3 Use your hand to firmly smooth it down.

4 Use any spare pieces of gold leaf to fill in any gaps.

21 Making glitter paper or card

With this technique you will get glitter all over you and probably all over the house, but it is a great way to get the perfect glitter card or paper. You can use most fine glitters and any smooth card or paper.

1 To protect your work area, put the paper face up inside a plastic tub or cardboard box. Shake the can of spray adhesive and spray all over the paper with a thin, even coat.

2 Transfer the sticky paper to a clean box, such as a clean food container, and sprinkle the glitter all over the paper.

3 Tip up the paper so the excess glitter falls into the box, tapping gently on the back to remove loose glitter.

4 Gently rub the paper to ensure that all the glitter on the paper is stuck. Lots of glitter will fall off, but an even coat should remain.

22 Making epoxy stickers

The pearly texture and shine of epoxy stickers is easy to imitate with a little help from the glue department. All you will need is a glue that dries clear and three-dimensional, so your sticker will retain its height and shape.

Punched shape

1 Punch out your chosen shape from thick card or paper (to make it self adhesive, first apply double-sided tape to the back).

2 Place the punched-out shape face up on a scrap of paper, then apply a thick coat of the dimensional glue to the shape.

3 If an air bubble forms, break it with a needle or the tip of a paper piercer while it's wet. Let it dry completely, following the manufacturer's instructions.

Stamped design

1 Stamp your chosen image using an ink pad filled with water-resistant ink (most dimensional glues are water based).

2 Colour, if necessary, using water-resistant colours.

3 Apply a thick coat of the dimensional glue over the stamped motif only. Remove any air bubbles and let it dry completely.

23 How to stamp

Stamping is a quick and easy way to add designs and colours. There are two types of motif stamps: outline and solid. The outline stamps are linear illustrations that, once stamped, you can colour in. The solid stamps are bolder, with no empty spaces to colour in. Always do a trial on a spare piece of the same card, or other surface, before stamping the final project.

1 Apply ink evenly to the stamp with an ink pad, holding the ink pad with one hand and dabbing it across the rubber stamp, held face up.

2 After applying the ink, hold the stamp with both hands and press down firmly and evenly.

3 To avoid smudging the motif, hold the paper firmly as you stamp

4 Trim the card to size after you have stamped the motif.

24 Cleaning stamps

A damp cloth will remove most inks, but use a stamp cleaner for permanent or very dark ink. Never put a stamp under running water because the glue that holds on to the motif may dissolve. Always clean your stamps before putting them away.

3 Stamp a motif over the background.

1 Clean the stamp carefully with liquid cleaner after using dark colours.

2 After cleaning, dry with a soft tissue, or alcohol-free baby wipes.

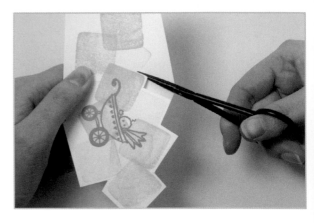

4 After you have stamped the motif trim the card to size.

25 Stamping with found objects

You can make stamps from many materials, as long as the surface will hold some ink. This example uses a soft, smooth eraser to make a square background.

1 Apply colour evenly to one side of a soft eraser.

26 Making a stamp

You can make stamps from many materials, as long as the surface will hold some ink. A simple eraser makes a great stamp – it's perfect: inexpensive, easy to find, soft and made from rubber

2 Stamp, then lift the eraser. Repeat to make your pattern.

1 Draw a simple motif with a soft lead pencil on paper (don't make it too detailed – you will have to cut it out).

2 Turn it over, then centre it on an eraser and scribble over the back of the motif to transfer it to the eraser.

3 Redraw the transferred lines to make them clearer.

4 Compare the image on the eraser with your original drawing to see if anything is missing.

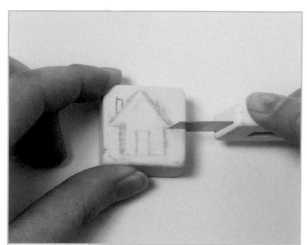

5 With a sharp craft knife, cut along the outlines to a depth of about 3mm (⅛in.).

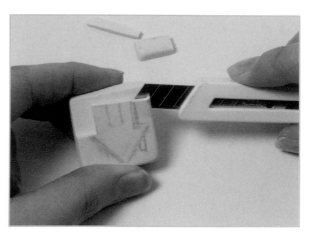

6 To remove the excess material around the outlined motif, cut into the side of the eraser.

7 Cut a shallow groove along each line within the main outline, such as the outline of the door above, so it will show on the final print.

8 Apply ink evenly to the stamp.

9 The finished stamp will be a mirror image of your original drawing. This is especially important to remember if your stamp contains lettering.

27 Embossing with stamps

Embossing a motif adds a gentle 3-D texture and a metallic shimmer. You can use any kind of stamp with embossing, but avoid intricate designs, which will not maintain their fine lines when embossed.

1 Apply embossing ink evenly to the stamp.

2 Press the stamp firmly onto a card, using both hands.

3 To catch excess embossing powder, place a large sheet of scrap paper under the card. While the ink is still wet, sprinkle a generous amount of powder over the motif.

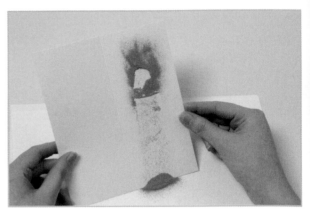

4 Tip up the card so the excess powder falls onto the paper.

5 Tap gently on the back of the card to remove loose powder.

6 Clean off any stray grains of powder with the tip of an orange stick or a fine-tip paintbrush.

7 Pour the loose powder on the scrap paper back into the box – you can use it again.

8 Gently heat the powder on the card with a heat gun.

28 Using a paper punch

Some paper punches easily cut through thin weights of card, so if you want punches for apertures, ask at your local craft shop for assistance or to try out the punch, with card as well as with paper before you buy. Punches do have one limitation: how deep they can punch.

1 On a folded card, turn the punch over and position it where you want the aperture.

2 Repeat, if you wish, to make several apertures.

29 Using a circle cutter

Circle cutters are wonderful tools that cut circles and apertures. You can place them in any position and they have a huge range of sizes. Different manufacturers produce different types of circular cutters: the one pictured here doesn't create a mark in the centre of the cutout so it is perfect for creating circular pieces of card.

1 Select the right size template and blade and position the template on the card, on top of a cutting mat. Cut around the template until the circle is complete.

2 Check that the circle has been cut all the way around, and lift it out to make the aperture.

30 Using a paddle punch

This type of punch makes a deep indentation in your cutting mat, so keep an old or special mat just to use with it.

1 To find the centre of your card, start by drawing a line at 45 degrees to the right side edge.

2 Draw another diagonal at 45 degrees to the left side edge. The lines intersect at the centre.

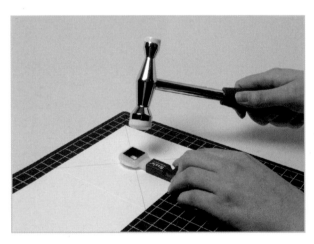

3 Centre your punch on the intersection, hold it steady and hammer the punch to punch out the hole.

4 Use this card as a template for making perfectly centred apertures every time.

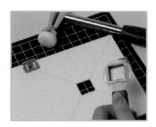

5 Repeat step 3. Put a card of the same size underneath it and secure it with paper clips.

31 Punches and die-cutting machines

Although they are mostly meant for punching paper, some will also cut card. There are many different designs in a variety of sizes and it is useful to have a selection.

1 Insert the paper into the punch and push down. Some punches need more pressure than others.

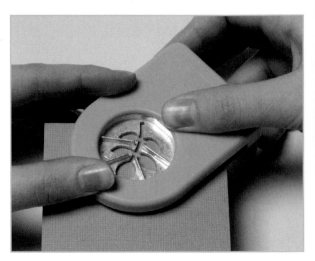

2 If you want to make a mirror image of the motif, turn the punch upside down, insert the paper and push down.

3 Use a tiny drop of PVA glue to attach a small punched-out shape.

32 Stencil embossing

Pierced metal stencils can be used again and again, so try to build up a collection of useful shapes.

1 Place a stencil on the front of a card or piece of paper, then secure it with low-tack tape.

2 Turn the card or paper over and place it on a light box or hold it against a window so you can see the design. If you are embossing card, apply a little soap – either from a bar or using a soapstone pencil as shown above – or rub through a sheet of waxed paper so a stylus will slide easier.

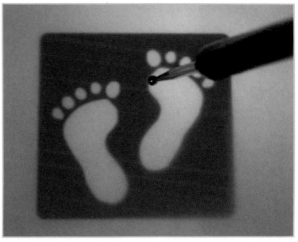

3 With the stylus, press gently around the edges of the design.

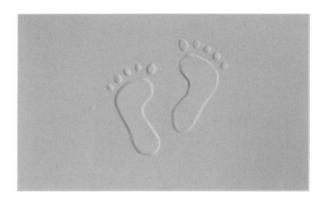

4 This is how the face of the design looks when embossed from the back. You may want to emboss certain projects from the front, which will give you a sunken instead of a raised design.

5 Lift a corner of the template to check the design. You can replace the template if something needs to be embossed again, or if you want to colour it in.

33 Colouring in stencils

One of the best ways of colouring an embossed card is by using craft chalk. These come in a wide range of different colours which you can blend.

1 Using a clip pen rub a cotton ball across the coloured chalk.

2 With the stencil still in position to protect the surrounding card, apply the chalk with a circular motion to the design.

3 Spray with fixative – hair spray will do – from about 40in. (100cm) away. Another way of colouring with chalk is to apply a watermark ink pad over the stencil once it is embossed, then colour (a similar technique is used on Engagement Announcement, pages 82–83).

34 Stamping onto clay

Stamps are not only for card or paper – some designs stamp beautifully on clay. The best ones for this have negative motifs (solid images with carved parts) that have clear edges so it is easy to know where to cut. This kind of stamp will create a positive raised motif on the clay, similar to the effect of dry embossing.

1 With most clays you will first need to prepare the material by kneading it with your hands until it is soft enough to flatten with a rolling pin.

2 Using the rolling pin, roll out the clay on a flat surface until it is smooth and about 2mm (¹⁄₁₆in.) thick.

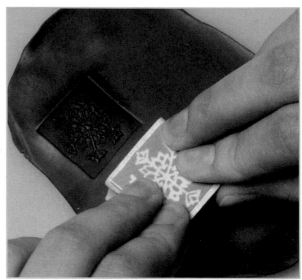

3 Check that the stamp is clean and dry, and then stamp the clay, just as you would stamp on paper. Press down firmly, then lift the stamp carefully.

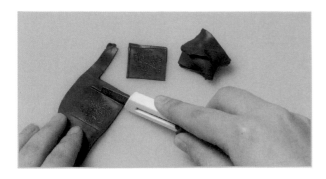

3 Press your chosen object firmly into the 'cookie,' making sure that it doesn't move around.

4 Using a craft knife, scissors or a cookie cutter, cut out the stamped motif.

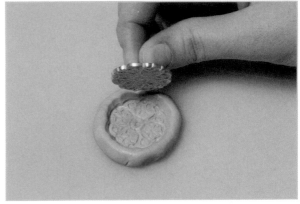

35 Making a mould

Another way of making clay embellishments is with your own moulds, made with buttons, seashells or any found objects with an attractive shape. A simple way to make the mould is by using silicone compound, but always read the manufacturer's instructions first.

4 Wait for a few minutes, then lift out the object leaving the pattern in the mould.

1 Take equal amounts of the two silicone components.

5 Now fill the mould with clay, pressing down gently to make sure that it fills every detail. Cut away any excess from the top to make it flat.

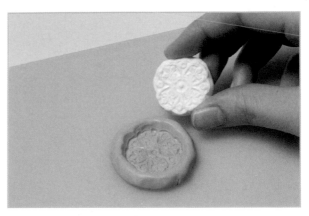

2 Mix them until you get an even colour, then form a ball. Squash the ball into a smooth cookie shape.

6 Remove the clay motif from the mould. It is now ready for baking, colouring or decorating.

36 Applying colour to clay

There are many ways to apply colour to the clay. Markers and craft chalk blend nicely with white clay, but make sure that the colouring materials are heat-resistant if the clay you are using needs to be baked. My favourite colouring medium is heat-resistant pigment powder.

1 Turn the pot of pigment over once or twice to coat the inside lid with a very thin coat of pigment. Rub your finger on it to pick up the perfect amount of powder (applying too much powder means you will lose some details from the stamped image).

2 Take your stamped and cut – but not dried – clay motif and dab some pigment powder on to it very, very gently. Remember, the more pressure you apply, the more detail you will lose.

3 If the clay needs baking, carefully follow the manufacturer's instructions. Sometimes even heat-resistant products change their colour a little.

37 Using gold foil on clay

Imitation gold leaf or foil is easy and affordable. Before it is dried, polymer clay is one of the materials that gold foil will stick to, so you will not need any glue. The colour of the clay will show through, so choose a clay that matches your colour scheme.

1 Roll out a piece of prepared polymer clay and apply a little gold foil.

2 With the tips of your fingers, rub the foil gently to ensure that it covers and adheres to the clay.

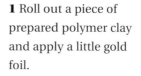

3 Choose a stamp with a bold motif, then stamp the foil-covered clay (see How to stamp, page 33).

4 With a craft knife, trim along the edges of the stamped motif.

5 With tweezers, pinch the edges gently to sharpen and define them, then bake the motif if necessary.

38 Rectangular inserts

These are the quickest and easiest type of insert to make.

1 To make an insert for a rectangular card, measure the inside of the card and then cut a piece of paper that is 9mm (⅜in.) shorter on each dimension.

2 Fold the insert in half, so it is ready to place inside the card.

3 Open the card and tuck the insert inside, aligning the fold lines, then apply a line of double-sided tape to the front of the insert.

4 Fold over the front of the card and press down gently so it sticks to the tape.

5 Open the card to find the insert ready for writing.

39 Vellum cards

In vellum cards the inserts will show through, so different techniques are needed.

1 When making an insert, it works best to centre it so it has a vellum frame all around. Start by folding the piece of insert paper in half, then cut it to the desired size.

2 If the front of the card has a decoration the adhesive attaching the insert will not show, in which case use double-sided tape.

3 Usually the adhesive will show through the translucent vellum. If so, once you have cut and folded the insert, apply vellum tape.

4 Rub the bone folder over the tape, then peel off the backing.

40 Aperture cards

Some aperture cards look better with a coloured card behind the hole, so the white insert does not show. You could make the insert from coloured paper, but it is difficult to write on darker colours unless you have the right pens. As an alternative you can make a smaller insert that will not show through the aperture.

1 After the aperture has been cut, open the card flat. Position the insert paper on top and mark the top edge of the insert below the aperture.

2 Cut the insert, fold it in half and attach it to the inside front of the card.

2 Position the square on the open card and mark the irregular sides, 5mm (³⁄₁₆in.) inside the edges of the card.

3 Mark the top and bottom of the score lines to match the fold lines of the card, and score the insert with a bone folder and ruler.

41 Irregular shapes

These are easy to make if you follow the simple steps shown here.

1 The best way to make a perfect insert when the card is not square or rectangular is to first cut a square that is 9mm (³⁄₈in.) shorter than the longest and widest dimensions of the card.

42 Stamping paper

You can create different patterns by experimenting with colour and position.

1 To stamp a motif in straight lines, position the stamp by eye or lightly mark a grid with a fine pencil first, then stamp each intersection.

2 Another regular pattern is the half-drop repeat. Each motif is centred between two in the row above.

3 Randomly stamping creates a spontaneous, lively look.

2 Add water until the bottle is almost full.

3 Screw on the top end and shake well until the water and powder are thoroughly mixed.

43 Making a colour spray

Another wonderful use of pigment powder is to make your own coloured spray, which you can use to make backgrounds on cards (see Baby Shower, pages 58–59) or to make wrapping paper.

4 Spray the card or paper. The closer you spray the more pigment will settle; if you spray from farther away, the effect is more subtle. Leave to dry.

1 Put a small amount of powder in an empty spray bottle.

5 Because there is no adhesive in the mixture, the finished result will need some kind of fixative. Spray the surface lightly from approximately 100cm (40in.) away.

44 How to wrap

Most crafters have a box full of scrap pieces of beautiful patterned paper, either leftovers from other present wrappings or just from craft projects. You can use these odds and ends to create a beautiful and unusual gift wrap.

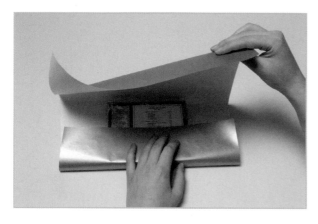

1 Cut the paper roughly to the size of the gift.

2 As you wrap, cut off any excess paper to keep the wrapping neat.

3 Use clear tape or, for neater joins, double-sided tape.

4 Trim the ends straight, leaving just enough to cover each end of the gift.

5 Fold over each corner, then neatly fold over the flap and trim it along the centre of the edge.

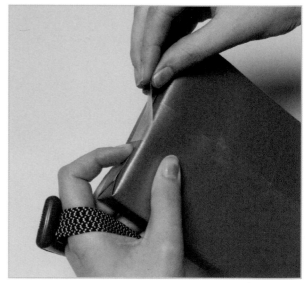

6 Secure each flap with tape.

7 Using double-sided tape, attach a wide strip of co-ordinating patterned paper around the wrapped gift.

8 Wind matching string, ribbon or thread around the gift.

10 Using double-sided tape, attach a piece of matching paper to cover the back.

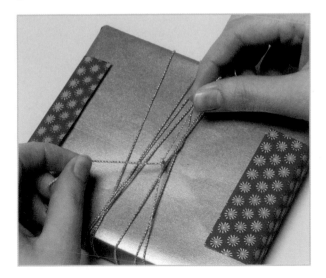

9 Knot the string at the back.

11 Attach a matching tag (see overleaf for instructions).

45 Punched tags

Tag-shaped punches provide an easy way to make perfect tags.

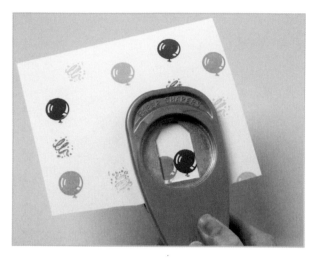

1 If you are working with patterned paper, turn the punch over to make it easier to select and punch the right section of the pattern.

2 Once the tag has been punched out, use a hole punch to make a hole for attaching it.

46 Double tags

These are easy to make with any shaped punch.

1 Fold a scrap piece of wrapping paper in half.

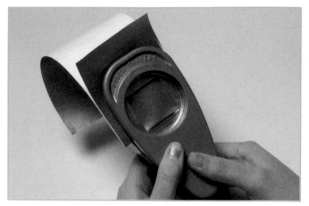

2 Punch out the shape, making sure the folded edge is inside the edge of the punch so it won't be cut. You can punch a hole through both layers, just one or none, as you like.

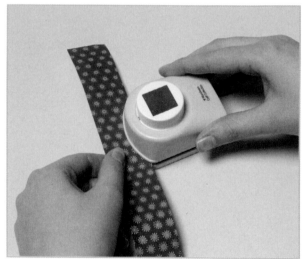

3 Punch out a shape from patterned paper.

4 Attach it, using double-sided tape, to the front of the tag.

47 Using a die-cutting machine

Some die-cutting machines have several different shapes that you can use to make a chain of tags. Each tag can have one word or one letter, to spell a sentence or just a name.

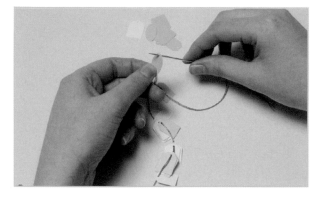

1 Using the die-cutter, make as many tags as you need from different coloured card, then stitch them together with matching thread, leaving the needle on.

2 Write the letters or words of the message on each tag. If you are not confident you will get it right the first time, write the tags before joining them.

3 Using the needle, stitch the chain of tags to the ribbon, then make a knot.

48 Using a template

Templates are a good way of getting a tag that is exactly the right size and shape.

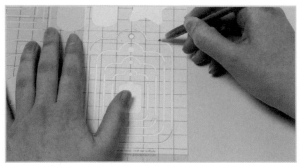

1 Place the template on the back of a card or piece of paper, then draw around it with a pencil (this way no difficult-to-erase pencil lines will be left on the front). Make a mark where the hole should go.

2 Cut around the pencil lines.

3 Punch the hole, then remove any remaining pencil lines with a soft eraser.

4 Decorate the tag to match the card or gift wrap, in this case by punching out three flowers.

5 Add the ribbon or thread (see Attaching fibres to a tag, page 29).

49 Using shipping tags

Ready-made shipping tags are very versatile. You can stamp them, punch them or use them to make a mini card.

1 Using masking tape, attach two tags together edge to edge.

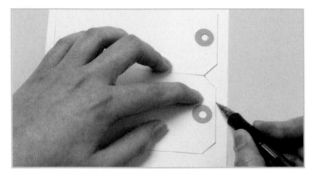

2 Place the joined tags on a piece of white paper, then draw around them to outline the insert.

3 Spray an even coat of adhesive onto the back of a piece of patterned tissue paper.

4 Position the tags, tape down, on the tissue paper, then use your hand to smooth it down.

5 Cut and fold the excess tissue paper to make a patterned edge all around the inside of the tag.

6 Using double-sided tape, attach the insert to the inside of the tag, trimming it so there is an even border.

7 Punch a hole through the completed, folded tag.

50 Square boxes

With this clever old method you can make a perfect square box with just a card, pencil, ruler, bone folder and scissors. You do not even need any adhesive.

1 Cut a piece of card into a square. With a pencil, draw two diagonal lines from corner to corner.

2 Using a bone folder, fold over each corner to the intersection of the pencil lines, then open it out.

3 Next, fold each corner to the intersection of the pencil line and the farthest fold line made in Step 2.

4 Turn the card over and fold the four flaps up to the closest fold line.

5 Cut two opposite flaps along the creases up to the last fold line, forming a house shape.

6 Fold in the sides along all the creases, leaving the house-shaped ends until last.

7 Fold in the house-shaped ends.

8 To make a lid for the finished box you will need to start with a piece of card that is 2mm (1/16in.) longer on each dimension. The method is the same as for making the box.

9 To make a ribbon handle you need to open out the assembled lid. Decide where you want to put the handle, in this case 2.5cm (1in.) from the scored line.

10 Draw two sets of parallel lines – about 6mm (¼in.) apart and slightly longer than the width of the ribbon – to mark where to cut.

11 Using a craft knife, cut the lines.

12 From the top, push the ribbon in and out through each cut, leaving a big loop of ribbon between the two sets.

13 Put the lid on the box, then tie the ribbon in a bow (see Red Valentine, pages 100–103).

14 Attach punched-out flowers onto the strips holding the ribbon. Add the tags (see Christmas Trees, pages 116–119). Trim the excess ribbon, making a V by folding it in half lengthwise, then cutting the ends diagonally.

51 Making boxes to measure

Making boxes to measure is easier with a scoring board.

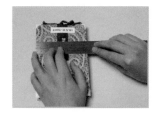

1 First, measure the length and width of the item.

2 Then measure the thickness of the item.

3 Find the closest groove in the scoring board that is slightly higher than the thickness of the item. Add twice that measurement to the length and width, then cut a piece of card to these dimensions.

4 Score the four edges of the card, using the groove you have found. Make two parallel cuts in the centre of the card to thread the ribbon through.

5 At each corner, cut the scored lines to the point where they intersect to make a flap. Fold over the edges along the scored lines.

6 Cut the flaps at an angle.

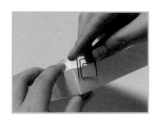

7 Using a wet glue, such as PVA, attach the flaps to the side and clamp them with paper clips while they dry.

8 From the top, push the ribbon in and out through the cuts in the centre.

9 To make a lid for the box, you will need to start with a piece of card that is 3mm (⅛in.) longer on each dimension. The method is the same for making the box. You can also punch a semicircle centred along two opposite sides, to make it easy to lift the lid off.

10 To make a nice bow for the box, wrap a ribbon around the ends of the box, twist them at the bottom, then wrap them over the sides and up to the top, slipping them under the ribbon as shown.

11 Make a knot, then tie the ribbon ends into a bow (see Red Valentine, pages 100–103).

52 Trunk box

This is a useful little box for party favours.

1 Cut a piece of light pink card measuring 16 x 15cm (6¼ x 5¾in.) and a piece of darker pink card measuring 10 x 8.5cm (4 x 3½in.).

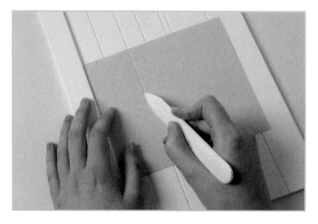

2 Score the four edges of the lighter card using the groove on the scoring board at 5cm (2in.). If you are not using a scoring board, measure 5cm (2in.) from the edges of the card, then score with a bone folder and ruler.

3 At each corner, cut the scored lines to the point where they intersect to make a flap.

4 Number the flaps in the order that you are going to fold them to make the box.

5 Using PVA glue, attach each side of the box and clamp with paper clips until it dries.

6 To make a lid for the finished box, repeat the method but cut out the squares in two corners on the same (front) edge.

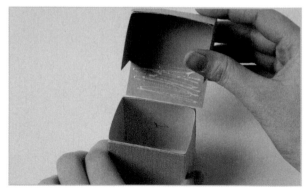

7 Glue any embellishments to the lid or box with PVA glue.

53 Party bags

Scoring templates designed specifically for bag making are wonderful. You can make a dozen party bags easily.

1 Cut a piece of paper then place it on the template and secure with paper clips.

2 Using a bone folder, score all the lines on the template.

6 Glue the sides together with a wet adhesive and clamp with paper clips.

3 Follow the instructions on the board and cut some of the scored lines (the darker lines on the board instruct you where to cut).

7 Leave the paper clips until the glue dries.

4 Fold over along the scored lines to create flaps.

8 Punch two holes through the top edge of each side, front and back. To make sure the holes align evenly and parallel, mark them before you glue the bag together. Alternatively, punch the front first, mark the inside of the back in pencil, then punch the back.

5 Cut notches in the flaps so the bag will close better.

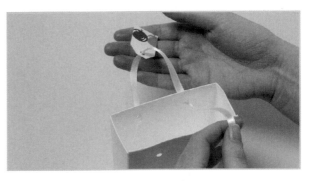

9 From the inside of the front, thread a ribbon out through one hole, through a tag, then back in through the other hole. Adjust the loop to the desired handle size, then knot each end to secure it. Repeat the method, omitting the tag, to make a handle for the back.

Projects

All these projects can be made as cards, invitations or thank-you notes – just add the appropriate wording inside. You can also make matching tags, gift wrap or boxes for any of the projects by following the instructions in the Basic Techniques section and using the design motifs and ideas featured in the project.

Baby Shower

The use of stickers here is an easy way of making lots of cards in record time, for very little money. Change the colour to a pale pink to announce that a girl is expected or perhaps a pale yellow when the sex is unknown.

You will need

Coloured, textured handmade paper
White thin card
Matching-coloured pigment ink pad
Baby-themed sticker
Silicone glue
Bone folder
Tweezers
Paper trimmer

1 Cut a piece of paper 2 measuring 5 x 10cm (2 x 4in.) and fold it in half lengthwise using the **bone folder 1**.

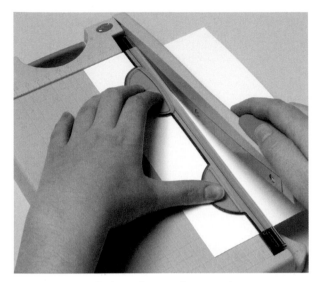

2 Cut a piece of white thin card measuring 10 x 7cm (4 x 2⅞in.).

3 Attach the baby sticker to the white card. If the sticker is a permanent type then place it on your hand to lose some of its tackiness before positioning it, as you will need to remove it from the card later.

4 Using a matching pigment ink pad, **ink over the edges** 23 of the sticker using uneven pressure each time.

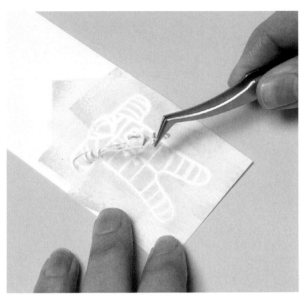

5 Using the tweezers, remove the sticker, leaving a white outline of it.

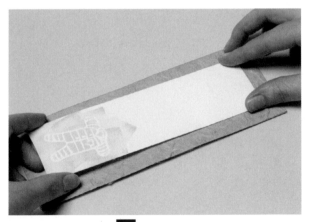

6 Centre, then **glue** 10 the card to the coloured textured card, blue is used here.

TIP

If you can't find an appropriate sticker for the masking stamp, then **emboss** 27 with white embossing powder. Apply the ink as in Step 4, then wipe the ink on top of the embossed parts with a tissue.

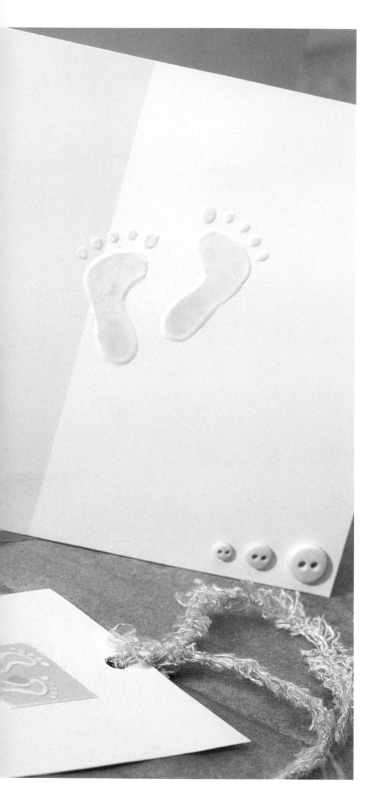

Birth Announcement

These long thin envelopes are great to use as cards, plus they fit into the more common DL size envelopes. If you like the idea but want to change the size, just make sure that the chosen size fits in an envelope.

You will need

Long, thin envelope
White card
Pink paper
Double-sided tape
White pigment ink pad
Rubber stamp
Fibres
Low-tack tape
Square punch
Hole punch
Scuffer or emery board
Paper trimmer or decorative scissors
Brass stencil
Stylus

1 Take a long, thin envelope measuring 21.5 x 8cm (8½ x 3⅛in.) and glue the flap down with its own glue or with **double-sided tape** **8** .

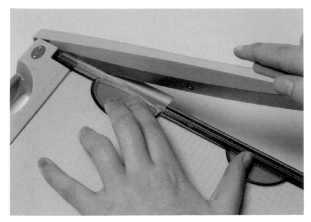

2 Trim a strip about 1cm (⅜in.) wide off one end, using a **paper trimmer** **2** or, for extra embellishing, decorative scissors.

3 Using white pigment ink, **stamp** **23** the feet motif all over the envelope.

5 Using low-tack tape, attach the brass stencil to the printed pink paper.

6 Emboss **32** the design.

4 Punch **28** a square aperture in the front towards the open end of the envelope (insert the top layer only into the punch and press down). Practise centring the aperture several times with similar-size envelopes to be sure of the exact position.

7 Punch out or trim the embossed design. If you have a smaller square punch than the one you used for the aperture, use it. Otherwise, just use the aperture punch first, then trim around the embossed design to make it a little smaller.

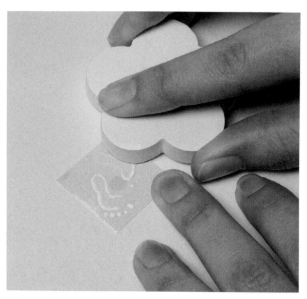

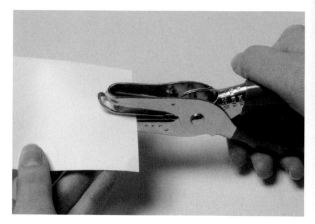

10 Slide the white card out of the envelope and punch a hole near the top edge, above the embossed image, so the fibres can be attached.

8 Using a scuffer or an extremely fine emery board, sand the embossed image, removing the printed layer so the white paper shows through.

11 Attach **17** the tie.

9 Cut a piece of white card 19.5 x 7.5cm (7¾ x 3in.) and slide it inside the envelope. Using double-sided tape, attach the embossed image to it, centring it inside the aperture.

Create matching tags for the new baby's gift. For instructions see pages 48–50. To create the alternative card also shown here, see **Embossing** **32** and **Colouring in** **33**

Children's Party

Children love interactive cards so why not spoil them with this circular motif. They will love twisting the top layer to read the inside. Choose a number stamp that corresponds with the birthday child's age and you have a perfect invitation or card.

You will need

Blue card

Yellow card

White smooth card

Six different coloured ink pads

Double-sided tape

Big brad

Circular cutter

Circle punch

Hole punch

Cutting mat

Rubber stamps

1 On the white card, randomly **stamp** 23 a balloon pattern using a selection of bright colour inks.

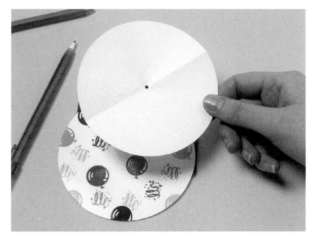

2 Using a different image, stamp between the balloons using the same colour inks.

5 To find the centre of the stamped card, cut a same-size circle from scrap paper. Fold it into quarters, then **pierce a hole** 18 where the fold lines intersect. Centre it on the stamped card, then punch a hole through the centre using a small **hole punch** 28 .

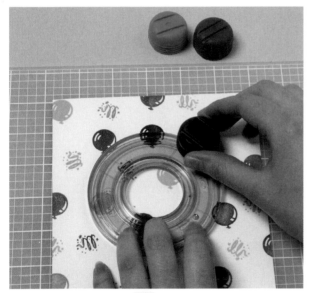

3 Using a **circle cutter** 29 , cut out a circle (use a size that fits in a standard square envelope).

4 Once it is cut, decide if the circle card needs more stamping.

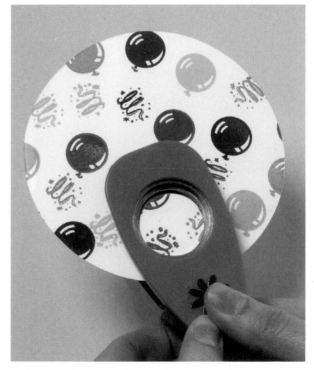

6 Using a circle punch, punch out a medium-size aperture near the edge.

7 From the blue card, cut a circle 2cm (¾in.) larger in diameter than the stamped card, then punch a hole through the centre.

8 Cut another circle from the yellow card, 1cm (⅞/16in.) smaller in diameter than the stamped card, then punch a hole through the centre. Using **double-sided tape** 8 , attach the yellow card to the blue one, aligning the centres.

TIP

When a bright and lively coloured background is required, use all six colours: yellow, orange, red, purple, blue and green. Combining these primary and secondary colours creates a happy rainbow.

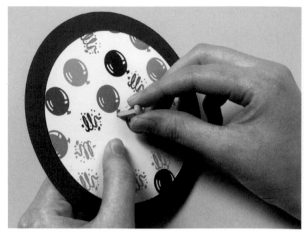

9 Place the stamped card on the yellow card, then secure all the layers with a **brad** 19 , so they rotate.

10 Write on the yellow card through the aperture, so when the stamped card is spun around the words will appear. Save a space to decorate with a stamped motif.

Make a matching party bag using the same balloon stamp. For instructions on how to make this bag, see **Party bags** 53 .

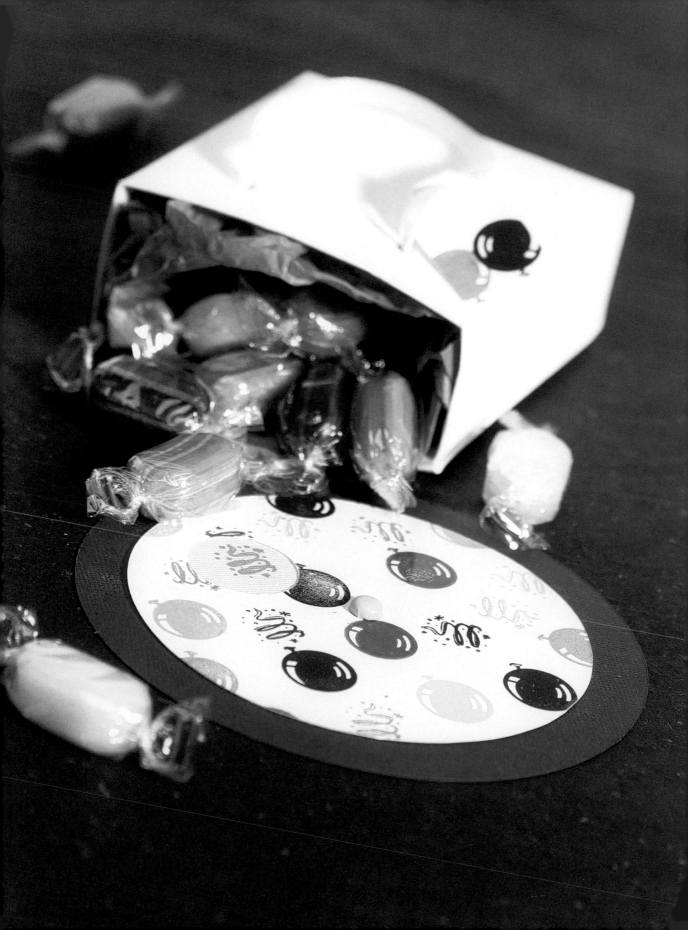

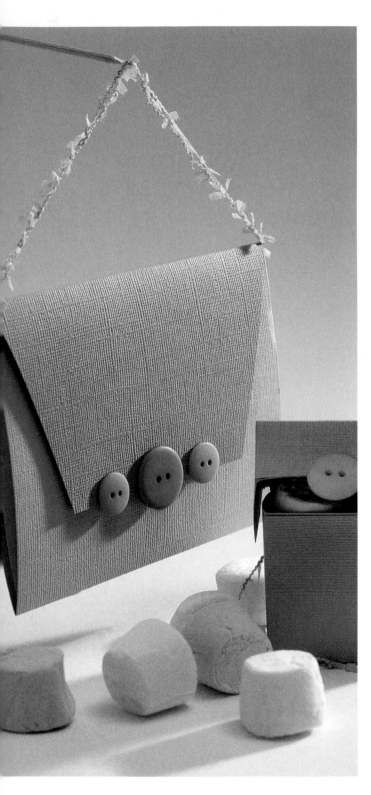

Pretty in Pink

This pretty purse card is perfect for an invite to a girly party and any little – or even grown-up – girl will love it. Think about changing the colour scheme to suit the colours of the party. Matching party-favour boxes make the event complete.

You will need

Dark pink card
Light pink card
Pink ribbon
Three pink buttons, in varying sizes
Double-sided tape
PVA glue
Ruler
Pencil
Cutting mat
Craft knife or guillotine
Bone folder

1 Measure and mark a piece of light pink card 21.5 x 15cm (8½ x 6in.) and a piece of dark pink card 15 x 15cm (6 x 6in.).

2 Using a guillotine or a craft knife and ruler, **cut** **2** out the cards.

3 Score **1** each card down the centre, then fold it in half.

4 On the dark pink card measure 2.5cm (1in.) from the corner and make a tiny mark with a pencil on each side of the longest edge.

5 Open out the dark pink card, then cut from the end of the centre fold to the pencil mark on each edge.

6 Cut a length of **ribbon** **15** 35cm (13½in.) long and tape the ends along the inside fold of the dark pink card.

7 Apply a strip of **double-sided tape** **8** along the top and bottom of the straight-sided section of the dark pink card, then peel off the backing.

8 Stick the light pink card to the dark pink card, so the fold of the light pink card is at the bottom and the flap of the dark pink card is at the top.

9 Glue a row of buttons to the edge of the flap with **PVA glue** **10**.

Make a matching **box** **52** for party treats using the same coloured card.

18th Birthday Party

Lace papers create beautiful, delicate backgrounds, and they come in an appealing array of patterns and colours. To really show them off, place them against a contrasting, coloured card.

You will need

Piece of dark blue card
Lace paper
Purple card
Velvet ribbon
Brad
Envelope
PVA glue
Sticky-dots tape
Silicone glue
Ruler
Pencil
Cutting mat
Craft knife
Cardboard box
Shaped punch
Spray glue

1 Cut **2** a piece of dark blue card to fit the envelope, then **fold** **1** it in half. Place the lace paper on top, then trim it roughly to size, leaving it bigger than the card.

2 Place the lace paper in the cardboard box and spray an even coat of **adhesive** **11** onto the back of it.

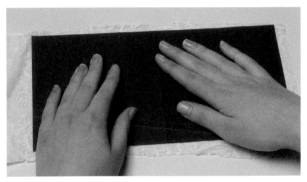

3 Position the card on the lace paper. Use your hands to smooth it down.

4 Turn the card over and trim the lace paper even with the card edges.

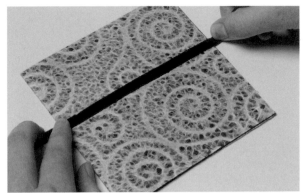

5 Using **sticky-dots tape** **9** , attach velvet ribbon across the front (this is normally a permanent method of fixing, but due to the texture of the ribbon, you can remove and reposition it if you like.

6 Punch **31** two flowers out of purple card and attach them with a tiny dot of **PVA glue** **10** in the centre. Using a paper piercer, make a hole and push a black **brad** **19** through.

7 Using **silicone glue** **13** , attach the flower to the velvet ribbon on the card front.

21st Birthday

By using double-sided patterned card you can make a card with a twist. Choose a pattern and colours to suit the woman or man who is celebrating the big day.

You will need

Double-sided patterned card
Eyelets
Coloured card
Fibres
Coloured paper
PVA glue
Pencil
Eraser
Metal-edged ruler
Craft knife
Bone folder
Scoring board
Eyelet setter
Hole punch
Cutting mat
Die-cutting machine
Hammer
Tweezers

1 Cut 2 a piece of double-sided patterned card 10 x 30cm (4 x 12in.), then **fold 1** in half widthwise, pattern side out.

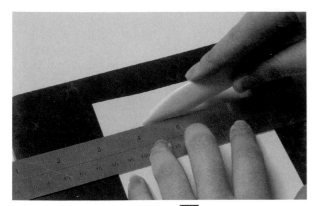

2 Using the bone folder, **score** [1] a line across the card 2.5cm (1in.) from the top edge, then fold it over.

3 Centre and set an **eyelet** [18] on each end of the folded section.

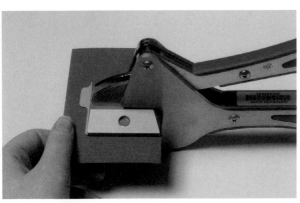

4 Die-cut [31] the numbers 2 and 1 out of the coloured paper.

5 Dab tiny drops of **PVA** [10] to the back of the numbers and glue them to the folded section using the tweezers.

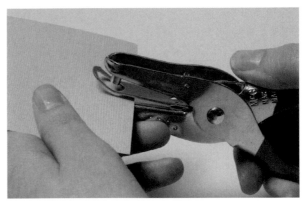

6 Cut a piece of coloured card, light brown here, 12.5 x 7.5cm (5 x 3in.) in size, then punch a centred hole near the top edge.

7 Add co-ordinating **fibres** [17].

For extra style, **wrap** [44] your gift with paper that matches the card.

Girls-Only Party

This is the perfect invitation or card for a special event, as it incorporates a bookmark to keep for posterity. Use it for a Hen Night, bachelorette party or a special birthday; this card is just right for any 'girls-only' occasion!

You will need

Pale pink card

Brown card

Sepia or brown ink pad

4.5mm (³⁄₁₆in.) eyelet

Fibres or embroidery floss

Corner punch

Eyelet setter

Hammer

Hole punch

Pencil

Eraser

Bone folder

Cutting mat

Craft knife

Paper trimmer

Card template (see page 125)

Metal-edged ruler

Rubber stamp

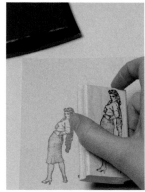

To make the bookmark

1 Stamp **23** the image onto the pale pink card using the sepia or brown ink pad.

2 Using the **paper trimmer** `2`, cut the card to 13 x 5cm (5⅛ x 2in.), then round the corners with the corner punch.

To make the card

1 Cut `2` a piece of brown card measuring 34 x 7.5cm (13⅜ x 3⅛in.) and **fold** `1` in half. Mark two parallel lines 10cm (4in.) from the fold and 1cm (⅜in.) from each edge.

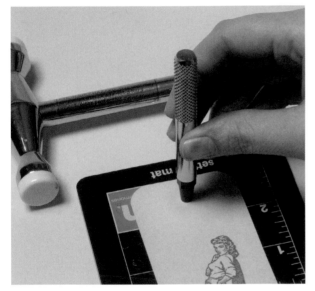

3 Punch a centred hole near the top edge, then insert and set an **eyelet** `18`.

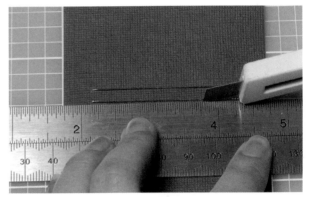

2 Using the craft knife, cut along each line to make two slits (for a template, see page 125).

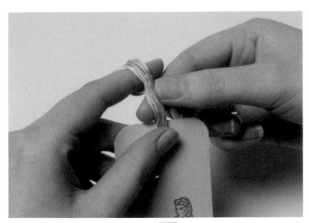

4 Add co-ordinating **fibres** `17`.

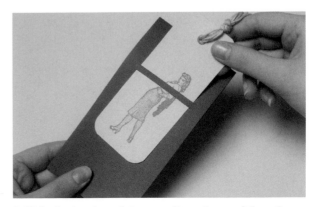

3 Slide the bookmark in one slit and out of the other.

Man's Birthday Card

It's often difficult to design cards for the men in our lives. Flowers are too feminine – anything cute or pretty doesn't do it. But this abstract pebble card is simple and masculine.

You will need

White card
Page pebbles in different sizes
PVA glue
Marble imitation gold leaf
Circle punch
Tweezers
Plastic tub

1 Take five page pebbles: one large, two medium and two small. Vertically centre the large one on the right side edge of the card, then create an interesting layout with the others.

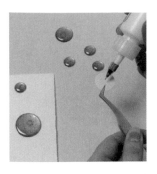

2 Remove the pebbles, one at a time so you do not forget the positioning, and use a little PVA glue to attach them to the card.

3 If you like, you can reposition a misplaced pebble slightly using tweezers, but do not push it too far, otherwise the glue will show.

Variation

1 Put the marble imitation **gold leaf** **20** face up in a plastic tub. Position each pebble on the gold leaf, sticky side down.

2 Press down firmly to make sure that the gold leaf adheres to the pebble.

3 Gently rub off the excess gold leaf (static may cause some bits of gold to stick to the top of the pebble, but they easily rub off).

4 Apply **PVA glue** **10** to the back of each pebble.

5 Onto a **three-aperture card** **28**, centre and glue the pebbles to the inside of the card through the apertures, so the positioning is perfect.

Graduation

With its mini mortar board, this simple, quick card is perfect for this special occasion. Use the card as an invitation to a graduation party or just to pass on congratulations.

You will need

Double-sided tape
White card
Black card
Black embroidery floss
Black eyelet
Pencil
Metal-edged ruler
Bone folder
Soft mat
Craft knife
Darning needle
Scissors
Setting mat
Eyelet setter
Hole punch
Hammer
Guillotine
Template (see page 125)

1 Cut **2** a piece of white card measuring 15 x 12.5cm (6 x 5in.), then **score** **1** it widthwise and fold it 10cm (4in.) from one end.

2 Cut a piece of black card measuring 5cm (2in.) square.

3 To find the centre of the black card, draw two diagonal lines, from corner to corner. The lines intersect at the centre.

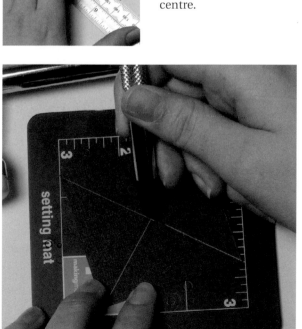

4 Make a hole in the centre and **attach an eyelet** 18 .

5 To make the tassel you will need to make a template (see page 125) from thick card. Wrap black embroidery floss lengthwise around the template.

6 When the tassel seems an appropriate thickness, tightly wind the floss around the strands (through the slot in the template) several times.

7 Using a darning needle, pull the floss under the wound floss.

8 Using the needle, slip a length of floss under the short top loops, then tightly tie it in a knot to make the top of the tassel (leave the ends of the tied floss untrimmed).

9 Cut through the long, bottom loops and trim them evenly.

10 Using **double-sided tape** 8 , secure the ends (only put tape on half of the card, since the other will show), then trim them.

11 Push the untrimmed floss ends through the eyelet.

12 Using double-sided tape on the same half, attach the black card to the white card so that half of the card extends beyond the edge of the white card.

Using the same colour scheme, **make a box** 51 for your graduation gift.

Engagement Announcement

A romantic stamped image helps you share the good news with your family and friends. These soft colours are perfect for a sweet, loving event, but you can punch them up for more drama if you prefer.

You will need

White card

Light green card

Two different shades of purple card

Watermark ink pad

Decorating chalk

Double-sided tape or sticky-dots tape

Pencil

Bone folder

Craft knife

Makeup applicators

Cutting mat

Soft eraser

Guillotine

Shaped stamp

1 Using the watermark ink pad, **stamp** **23** the image onto the piece of white card, then let it dry.

2 Using a makeup applicator, apply the chalk (the colour will be stronger across the stamped image).

3 Using a soft eraser, remove any unwanted chalk.

6 Fold and cut a piece of pale green card measuring 15cm (6in.) square. Draw two angled shapes to overlap the pale green card, each on a different shade of purple card.

7 Cut out the purple shapes, then attach them to the green card with **double-sided** 8 or **sticky-dots tape** 9 .

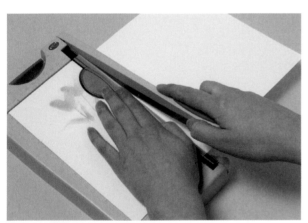

4 Trim 2 the white card to about 7.5cm (3in.) square.

5 Using the makeup applicator and chalk, **colour the edges** 6 .

8 Turn the card over, then trim the purple card even with the green card's edges. Using double-sided or sticky-dots tape, attach the stamped card.

Use the same flower stamp on a **gift tag** (see pages 48–50).

Engagement Party

A solitaire diamond ring makes this engagement announcement really sparkle. Using silver-coloured wire and clear crystals, you will be able to create cards that really suit the occasion.

You will need

White card

Patterned or decorative paper

Silver-coloured wire

Clear crystal

Double-sided tape

PVA glue

Silicone glue

Sticky-dots tape

Pencil

Tweezers

Bone folder

Scoring board

Wire cutters

Applicator stick

1 Fold and **cut** **2** a piece of white card measuring 11.5 x 17cm (4⅝ x 6⅞in.) when folded. **Score** a line about 5cm (2in.) from the left edge using the **bone folder** **1**.

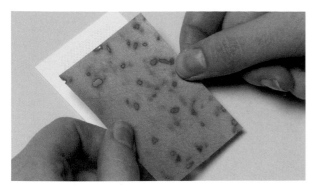

2 Cut a piece of patterned paper measuring 7 x 5cm (2⅞ x 2in.) and a same-sized piece from the white card, stick them together using **sticky-dots tape** 9 .

3 Using **double-sided tape** 8 , attach the left side edge of the patterned paper to the card front.

4 To make the ring, cut a length of silver-coloured wire, gently grasp it at the midpoint, then twist the two ends together.

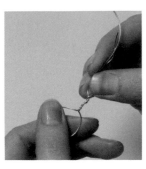

5 If the ring is too big, keep twisting the wires until it is the correct size.

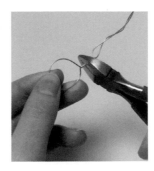

6 Using the wire cutters, cut the excess wire off.

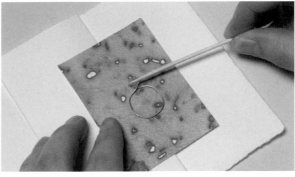

7 Centre and glue the ring to the card front with tiny drops of **PVA** 10 (place a heavy object on top until it dries).

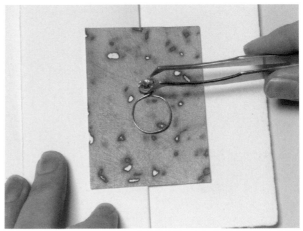

8 Attach the crystal with a dab of **silicone glue** 13 .

White Wedding

The transparency of vellum suggests delicate bridal fabrics. You can make this a really simple design in large quantities and in record time.

You will need

Vellum card
Lacy white ribbon
Silver brads
PVA glue
Bone folder
Soft mat
Paper piercer
Scissors
Vellum
Die-cutting machine
Flower die-cuts

1 Cut **2** a piece of **vellum card** **39** measuring 17 x 24cm (6¾ x 9½in.), then **fold** **1** it in half.

2 Glue on the white **ribbon** `15` with tiny drops of **PVA adhesive** `10`.

3 Turn the card over, then trim the ribbon even with the card edges.

4 Using the **die-cutting machine** `31`, punch out two different sized white flowers, then position them on the card. Using a paper piercer, make a hole through the flowers, ribbon and card front, then insert a **brad** `19`.

5 Attach a brad, turn the card over and separate and flatten the metal prongs on the back. To make an insert for this card see page 45.

Use the same white card and vellum to make a box and matching tags (see pages 48 and 52–54).

Wedding Folder

There are so many bits and pieces to include with a wedding invitation that a small folder is great to hold them all neatly. The patterned paper used here is actually a wrapping paper, but you can use any paper or even make your own.

You will need

Pale blue card
Matching patterned paper
Two co-ordinated big brads
Fibres
Sticky-dots tape
PVA glue
Pencil
Eraser
Metal edged ruler
Bone folder
Scoring board
Rectangular hole punch
Scissors
Two different sized circle punches

1 Cut 2 a pale blue card measuring 29.5 x 21cm (11⅝ x 8¼in.). **Score 1** lines 5cm (2in.) from the right edge and 10.5cm (4⅛in.) from the left edge of the card. Fold the card along the scored lines.

2 Cut two pieces of patterned paper, one measuring 20 x 9.8cm (7⅞ x 3⅞in.), the other 20 x 4.4cm (7⅞ x 1¾in.). With **sticky-dots tape** 9 , attach each to the corresponding card flap.

6 At each mark, punch out a tiny rectangle.

7 Place a punched circle over the punched hole in each flap and fasten it with a **brad** 19 .

3 Punch 28 out two tiny rectangles, not too close together, through a piece of the same pale blue card.

8 Apply a fine line of **PVA adhesive** 10 along each short edge of the small flap.

4 Turn the circle punch over, insert the punched card, centre the circle over a rectangle, and then punch.

9 Using your fingers, hold down the edges until the glue dries.

5 Find the centre of the card, then make a mark about 2.5cm (1in.) from the edge of each flap.

10 Put the invitation, envelope and RSVP card in the folder, then close the folder and wind the fibres around the brads.

Make a matching favour **box** 50 .

25th Anniversary

This card can easily be adapted for any kind of anniversary, even a birthday, with a few changes of colours and numbers.

You will need

White card
Silver organza ribbon
Silver ink pad
Silver paper
PVA glue
Pencil
Metal-edged ruler
Craft knife
Cutting mat
Background splatter rubber stamp
Die-cutting machine
Number die-cuts

1 Using the silver ink pad, **stamp** 23 the splatter pattern onto a folded piece of white card measuring 12.5cm (5in) square.

2 Position the silver **organza ribbon** **16** on the front of the card, then mark the top and bottom at each side of the stamped area.

5 Die-cut **31** the numbers 2 and 5 out of the silver paper.

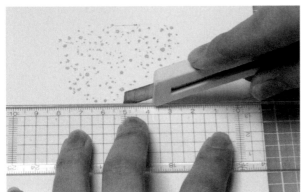

3 Using the craft knife, **cut** **2** a slot between each pair of marks.

6 Glue on the numbers using very tiny drops of **PVA glue** **10**.

4 From the front, push the ribbon in and out through the slots.

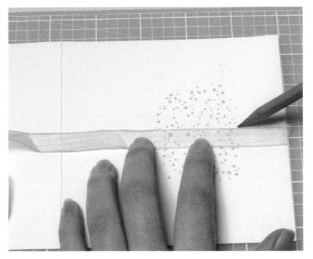

7 Tie the two ends of the ribbon in a decorative knot, and diagonally trim the ends.

50th Anniversary

A tiny gilded tile symbolises the solid, precious marriage that this golden anniversary celebrates.

You will need

Ivory card

Gold ribbon

White clay

Gold-leafing pen

Sticky-dots tape

Silicone glue

Scissors or craft knife

Rubber stamp

Rolling pin

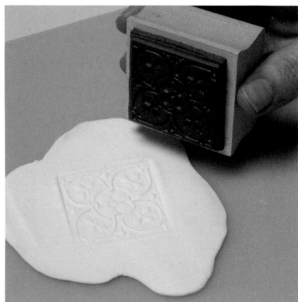

1 Using the rolling pin, roll out the clay on a flat surface until it is smooth and about 3mm (⅛in.) thick. Then **stamp** **34** it.

2 Using the scissors or craft knife, cut out the stamped motif and let the clay dry. If the clay needs to be baked, follow the manufacturer's instructions.

4 Using the **sticky-dots tape** 9 , attach the gold ribbon to the front of the ivory card. Then turn the card over and trim the ribbon ends even with the card edges.

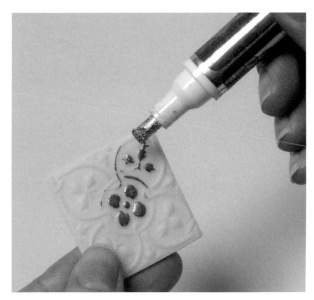

3 Holding the motif at an angle of about 45 degrees, **colour** 36 the raised areas of the motif using the gold-leafing pen.

5 Using the **silicone glue** 13 , attach the motif to the ribbon.

Tuck the card under the perfect bow on your gift (see Red Valentine, To make the bow, page 102, for instructions).

New Home

Keys and wallpaper are two things that any new home owner will have to contend with! Send congratulations with this card or send an announcement to friends and family, giving your new address.

You will need

Gray card

Patterned paper

Key charm

Silver-leafing pen

Silver cord

Double-sided tape

Double-sided foam tape

Pencil

Metal-edged ruler

Bone folder

Tweezers

Craft knife

Cutting mat

Scissors

1 Fold and **cut** **2** a piece of gray card 13.5 x 10cm (5⅜ x 4in.). Make a mark 3.5cm (1½in.) from the top on both the left and right side edges.

2 Using the craft knife and ruler, cut a line from the top edge to the mark on the left side edge.

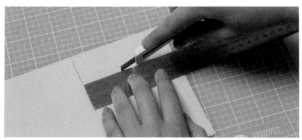

3 Then cut from the mark on the left side edge to the mark on the right side edge.

4 Using the silver-leafing pen, **colour** 5 both the top and right side edges of the card front.

5 Cut a panel of gray card measuring 10 x 4.5cm (4 x 1⅞in.), then colour the edges with the silver-leafing pen.

6 Cut a piece of patterned paper slightly smaller than the silver-edged panel. Using **double-sided tape** 8 , attach the patterned paper to the panel.

7 Thread the silver cord through the key charm, wrap it around the panel, and tie a knot on the back.

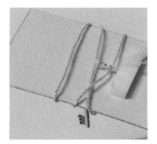

8 Stick two strips of double-sided foam tape onto the bottom two-thirds of the back of the card.

9 Inside, attach an **insert** 38 with double-sided tape.

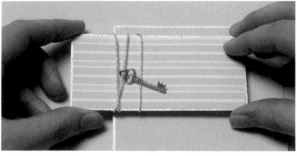

10 Attach the panel to the front of the card so the top third extends beyond the top edge.

At Home

Invite your friends for dinner or a traditional afternoon tea party using this elegant card. It also makes a delightful thank-you note if you have been the guest.

You will need

White vellum card

Silver paper

White card

Sticky-dots tape

PVA glue

Bone folder

Tweezers

Utensil-shaped punch

1 Cut a piece of the **vellum card** `39` measuring 21 x 15cm (8½ x 5⅞in.). Using the **bone folder** `1`, score two lines about 5cm (2⅛in.) from each end of the card then fold them over.

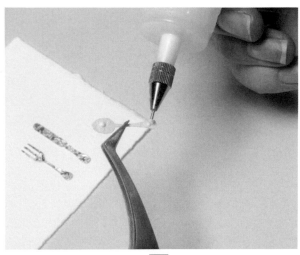

3 Using tweezers and **PVA** `10`, glue the shapes onto a piece of **deckle-edge** `3` white card measuring 9 x 7.5cm (3⅛ x 3in.).

2 Punch `28` cutlery shapes from the silver paper.

4 Using **sticky-dots tape** `9`, attach the white card to the vellum card.

TIP

It is not always easy to position a small item in the perfect place. Try arranging them (without glue) on the card first, then stick them on, one by one, while the others are in place.

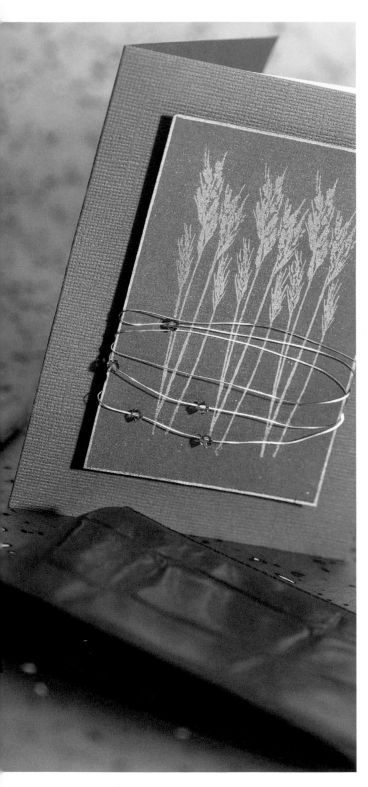

Retirement

Send your good wishes for happy new days of relaxation to a friend or colleague who is beginning an active retirement.

You will need

Brown card

Metallic pigment powder

Fixative spray

Gold-leafing pen

Gold wire

Crystal beads

Double-sided foam tape

Metal-edged ruler

Bone folder

Two soft paintbrushes

Craft knife

Cutting mat

Pliers

Watermark stamp

1 Onto a piece of brown card cut to your chosen size, **stamp 23** a centred image using the watermark pad, then stamp again on either side.

2 Using a dry soft paintbrush, apply the metallic pigment powder all over the images (hold the brush vertically and dab the powder, rather than brushing it on).

3 Using the second dry soft paintbrush, remove the excess powder (the powder will only adhere where the ink was stamped).

4 Holding the card about 40cm (15in.) away, spray an even coat of fixative.

5 Using the gold-leafing pen, **colour the edges 5** of the stamped panel.

6 Thread five amber crystal beads onto the gold wire.

7 Leaving the ends at the back, wrap the wire around the stamped panel.

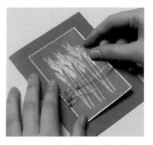

8 Using **double-sided foam tape 8** , attach the panel to a prepared, matching card (using foam tape ensures that you won't feel the wire inside the card).

Use the same stamp to make matching tags and gift wrap (for instructions, see pages 48–50).

Red Valentine

Whether you need an invitation for a Valentine's party or a love letter for someone special – make it romantic.

You will need

Red card
White card
Red watercolour ink
Black permanent ink pad
White ribbon
Double-sided tape
3-D glue
Pencil
Soft eraser
Metal-edged ruler
Bone folder
Scoring board
Two slots anywhere punch
Paper trimmer
Craft knife
Cutting mat
Scissors
Template (see page 124)
Rubber stamp

1 Cut 2 a piece of red card measuring 29.5 x 18cm (11½ x 7½in) then **score 1** two fold lines, each 10cm (4in) from opposite ends of the card, using the bone folder.

2 Make a mark 8cm (3¼in) from the top edge on each end of the card.

3 Trim off each top corner, cutting from each mark to the closest scored line where it meets the top edge.

4 Turn the card over and find the centre, then make a mark 7.5cm (3in) from the bottom edge.

5 Using an anywhere punch, make two holes through the back of the card only, over the mark. If you don't have a punch like this, you can measure and cut the slots with a craft knife instead.

6 From the back, push the white **ribbon** `14` in and out through the two slots as shown. Erase any pencil marks using the soft eraser.

7 Using the black permanent ink pad, **stamp** `23` a motif onto a piece of white card measuring 16.5 x 9cm (6½ x 3½in). Use the positional template (see page 124), or stamp on the card, and trim it to fit inside the red card.

8 Colour `22` the stamped motif with the red watercolour ink, then let it dry.

9 Apply 3-D glue `22`. Let it dry completely.

10 Centre the white card on the red card. Attach it using **double-sided tape** `8`, or leave it loose so that it can slide in and out.

To make the bow

1 Knot the two ends of the ribbon at the centre of the card front.

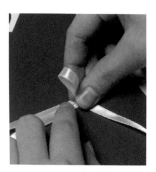

2 Make a loop with one end.

4 Knot the two loops to secure the bow.

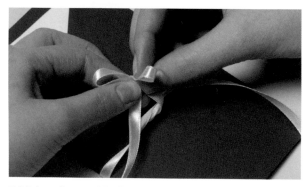

3 Make a loop with the other end, then tie a bow.

5 Cut a V in each ribbon end by folding it in half lengthwise and cutting away from the fold at a 45-degree angle.

Use the same stamp and repeat Steps 7 to 9 to make a matching tag for a gift to go with your card (see pages 48–50).

TIP

If you need to make many cards like this one, a stamping template makes positioning the motif faster, easier and more accurate.

With Love

Feathers are sophisticated, subtle and feminine. They want to float and fly, so they are not the easiest things to attach, but they make any card special, especially for Valentine's Day.

You will need

Jade card

Pink feathers

Pink paper

PVA glue

Silicone glue

Corner punch

Scoring board

Pencil

Soft eraser

Bone folder

Cutting mat

Metal-edged ruler

Tweezers

Heart-shaped punch

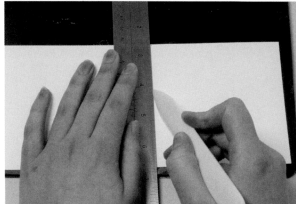

1 Cut **2** a piece of jade card measuring 30 x 10cm (12 x 4in.), then **score** **1** a line 10cm (4in.) from the left end and another line 5cm (2in.) from the right end. Fold it along the scored lines to make a gatefold.

2 Using the corner punch, round the corners of the card.

3 Mark the centre of the card in pencil, close to the edges.

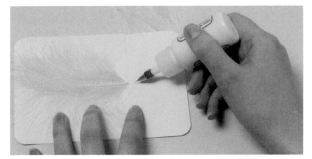

4 Glue on the feathers with **PVA adhesive** **10** (apply a line of glue along each pencil mark, then position the feathers on top).

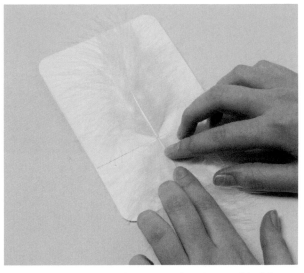

5 Gently press the feathers into the glue and hold until they dry.

6 Punch **28** out two different-sized hearts from the pink paper, then attach with **silicone glue** **13** , one to each fold of the card using tweezers.

Easter Eggs

A row of ready-made tags dotted with pretty pastel eggs dresses up this sweetly seasonal card.

You will need

Five white tags
Coloured paper
Coloured inks
Card blank
White thread
Masking tape
Self-adhesive foam dots
Bone folder
Tweezers
Double-sided foam tape
Egg-shaped punch
Soft eraser

1 String white thread through each tag and knot, then trim the ends.

2 Using masking tape, join the five tags edge to edge.

3 Using the soft eraser and the coloured inks, randomly **stamp** 23 and 25 .

4 Punch 28 out several eggs from the different coloured paper.

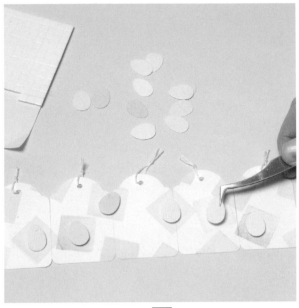

5 Using **self-adhesive dots** 12 , attach the eggs to the tags, sticking each egg onto a contrasting colour tag.

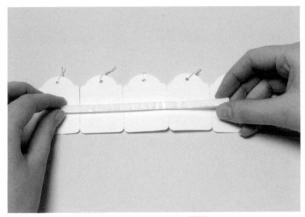

6 Using **double-sided foam tape** 8 , attach the tags to the front of the blank card. You could also make extra tags for Easter baskets.

Fourth of July

Celebrate American independence with a Fourth of July barbecue, and invite your friends and family with this card. Change the colours of the ribbon to suit the flag of your country.

You will need

White card

Blue ribbon

Red ribbon

Blue and red paper

Self-adhesive foam dots

Sticky-dots tape

Pencil

Eraser

Bone folder

Tweezers

Craft knife

Cutting mat

Scissors

Star shaped punch

1 Apply a strip of **sticky-dots tape** **9** along the back of a piece of the red ribbon.

2 Attach the ribbon to the front of a piece of white card measuring 14 x 11cm (5⅝ x 4¼in.) when folded in half.

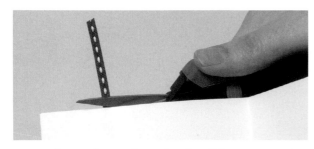

3 Turn the card over, then trim the ribbon even with the card edges.

4 Attach the blue ribbon perpendicular to the red, then attach another piece of blue ribbon parallel to the red.

5 Finally, attach another piece of the red ribbon perpendicular to the red, to create a woven effect.

6 Punch 28 out several stars from blue and red paper.

7 Apply self-adhesive dots to the back of the stars, then attach them to the card.

Halloween

Hanging a grinning jack-o-lantern in a dark circular window is simple to make and creates a fun, scary Halloween card.

You will need

Black card
Orange card
Yellow vellum
Green brush marker
Black thread
PVA glue
Sticky-dots tape
Pencil
Soft eraser
Circle cutter
Scissors
Die-cutting machine

1 Using the **die-cutting machine** **31** , cut out two jack-o-lanterns (if you are using textured card, turn the card over for one lantern, so you will have a textured front and back.

2 Carefully push out the perforated sections of the lanterns.

6 Glue black thread to the back of the other lantern with **PVA** 10 , then stick both lanterns together, textured side out if using textured card.

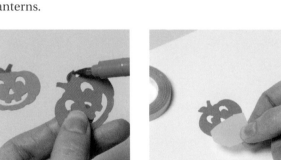

3 Using the green brush marker, paint the leaves on the top.

4 Using the **sticky-dots tape** 9 , attach the back of one lantern to a piece of yellow **vellum** 39 .

7 Using the **circle cutter** 29 , punch an aperture in a black card measuring 14.5 x 11cm (5⅝ x 4¼in.) when folded. Hang the jack-o-lantern from the thread to check which way it turns.

5 Trim the vellum even with the lantern edge.

8 When you are happy with its position inside the card, glue the thread above the aperture with PVA, then trim the thread even with the card edge.

Thanksgiving

Invite your friends and family for a traditional Thanksgiving dinner. Remind them what they'll be eating with the turkey stamp! The invitation can also be used as a menu.

You will need

Terracotta card

White card

Sepia ink pad

Watermark ink pad

Water-soluble coloured pencils

PVA glue

Pencil

Soft eraser

Bone folder

Metal-edged ruler

Paper trimmer

Tweezers

Craft knife

Cutting mat

Circle punch

Water brush

Rubber stamp

1 Cut 2 a piece of terracotta coloured card measuring 14cm (5½in.) square.

2 With a pencil, draw two diagonal lines from corner to corner.

3 Fold each corner to the intersection of the pencil lines.

4 Using the soft eraser, remove the pencil marks.

5 Using the watermark ink pad, randomly **stamp** `23` the turkey motif all over the outside of the card.

6 Using the sepia ink pad, stamp the same motif on a piece of white card.

7 Using water-soluble coloured pencils, **colour** `22` the motif.

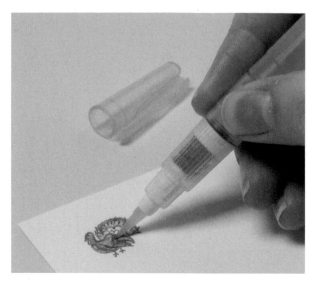

8 With the water brush, blend the colours (if you don't have a water brush, use a wet fine-tip paintbrush).

10 Using the sepia ink pad, colour the edges of the decorated punch-out.

9 Using the **circle punch** 28 , punch out the stamped motif.

11 Make an **insert** 38 , then add your desired text (for ideas on fonts and suggestions for the text layout, see pages 16–19). After attaching the insert, glue on the decorated punch-out with **PVA** 10 .

Christmas Trees

Send your best Christmas wishes in a card with a decorated tag that's designed to be detached and hung on a tree.

You will need

Green pearlescent card
White card
Green pearlescent ribbon
Green watercolour paint
Embossing powder
Watermark ink pad
Gold-leafing pen
Self-adhesive velcro dots
Bone folder
Craft knife
Cutting mat
Scissors
Paper trimmer
Corner punch
Rubber stamp with tree motif

1 Stamp and **emboss** **27** the trees motif on a piece of white card.

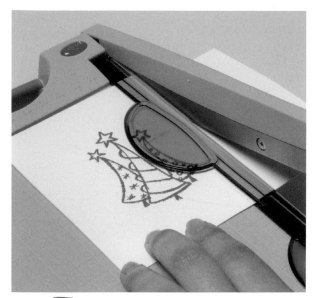

2 Trim **2** the embossed motif to size for the tag (a little smaller than the Christmas card).

3 Using the green watercolour paint, only **colour** **5** the central tree.

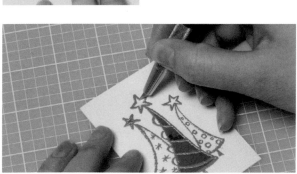

4 Using the craft knife, cut out inside the outlines of the three stars.

5 Using the corner **punch** **28**, round the corners of the tag.

6 Using the gold-leafing pen, colour the edges of the tag.

7 Fold the green pearlescent ribbon in half, then push the ends through the central star. Leave a loop at the top.

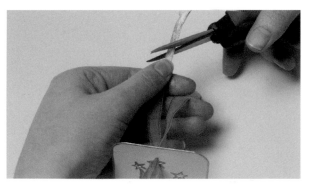

8 Cut a V in each ribbon end by folding it in half lengthwise, then cutting away from the fold at a 45-degree angle.

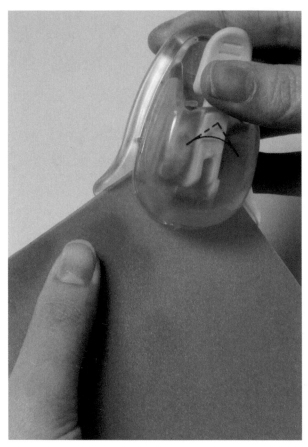

11 Attach four **self-adhesive Velcro dots** **12** to the back of the embossed tag, avoiding the cut-out stars.

9 Cut the green pearlescent card so it measures 17 x 11cm(6¾ x 4¾in.) when folded. Using the corner punch, round the corners.

10 Using the gold-leafing pen, colour the edges.

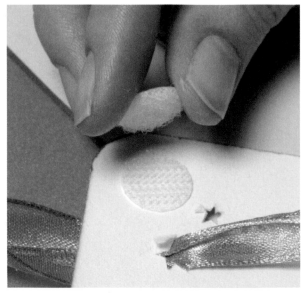

12 Attach the tag to the green card, gently pressing down on the Velcro dots. The Christmas tree tag also makes a festive gift tag.

Christmas Presents

For all children who celebrate Christmas, it's a magical time and a time for lots of presents. Any child will delight in this card that delivers its own tiny packages.

You will need

Red card

Gold leaf

Blue and red clay

Gold thread

Silicone glue

Double-sided adhesive sheet

Pencil

Soft eraser

Bone folder

Craft knife

Cutting mat

Paper trimmer

Scissors

Rolling pin

1 Using the rolling pin, roll out the blue polymer clay on a flat surface until it is smooth and about 3mm (⅛in.) thick, then sprinkle some gold-leaf flakes on top.

2 Roll over the clay to ensure that all the flakes are stuck down.

3 Using the craft knife, cut different-size squares and rectangles out of the clay. Follow Steps 1 to 3 with the red clay.

4 Dry or bake the clay, following the manufacturer's instructions, wrap the gold thread around each 'present,' and knot the ends at the back.

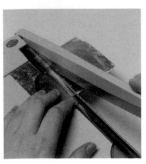

5 Using the double-sided adhesive sheet, make a **gold-leaf** 20 background, then cut it down to 4 x 6.5cm (1½ x 2½in.).

6 Peel off the backing and attach the gold-leaf background to a cut piece of textured red card measuring 17 x 7cm (6⅜ x 2¾in.) when folded in half.

7 To position the gold-leaf background correctly, peel back the top 1cm (⅜in.) across the backing, position it over the card and when satisfied, press along the adhesive. Peel off the remaining backing and press the background into place.

8 Using **silicone glue** 13 , attach the presents.

TIP

Short of time? No polymer clay? Substitute squares of wrapping paper. They won't create the same 3-D effect, but they are just as decorative.

Glittery Snowflakes

Whether it's an elegant evening dinner party or a New Year's cocktail party, this invitation adds glamour to winter entertaining.

You will need

White vellum card
White thin card
Light blue thin card
Glitter
PVA glue
Self-adhesive foam dots
Spray adhesive or vellum tape
Sticky-dots tape
Pencil
Soft eraser
Bone folder
Metal-edged ruler
Tweezers
Craft knife
Cutting mat
Paper trimmer
Snowflake-shaped punch

1 Cut **2** a piece of **vellum card** **39** measuring 17 x 12cm (6¾ x 4¾in.) when folded in half.

2 Using white and light blue thin card, make pieces of **glitter paper** **21**, then cut the white piece to 17 x 12cm (6¾ x 4¾in.).

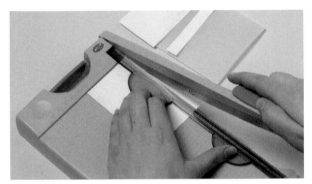

3 Cut three pieces of glitter paper in different widths.

4 Apply **spray adhesive** **11** or vellum tape to the back of the glitter pieces.

5 Stick the glitter pieces on the front of the card.

6 Punch **28** out three snowflakes from each glitter paper, and from the vellum card.

7 Glue the snowflakes together with **PVA** **10** (a drop in the centre should be enough).

8 Using **self-adhesive dots** **12**, attach the snowflakes to the card (attach the centre snowflake first, making it easier to position the other two).

Templates

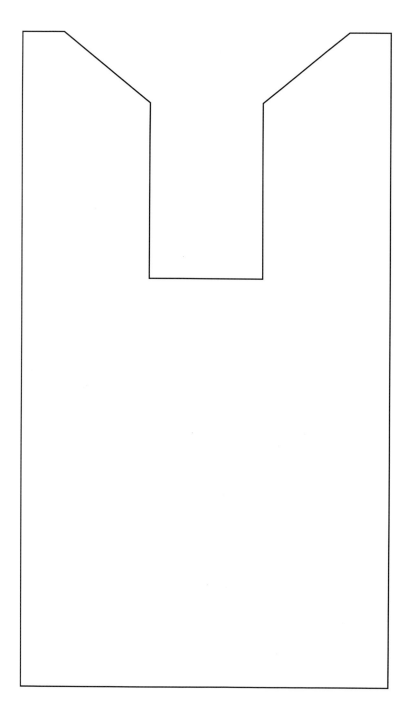

Red Valentine, used on pages 100–103

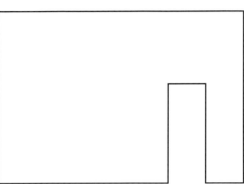

Graduation, used on pages 78–81

Girls-Only Party, used on pages 74–75

Suppliers

UK

Art-Kure Watercolour System
Hayloft Studios
Bellamarsh Barton
Kingsteignton Road
Chudleigh
Devon TQ13 0AJ
Tel: 01626 859100
http://www.art-kure.com
Manufacturers and distributors of the Art-Kure watercolour and stamping systems.

Artoz Ltd
Tannery Court Business Centre
Knight Road
Strood
Rochester
Kent ME2 2JH
Tel: 01634 722060
http://www.artoz.co.uk
Manufacturers and distributors of a wide range of papers, cards and embellishments.

Card Inspirations
The Old Dairy
Tewin Hill Farm
Tewin
Welwyn
Herts AL6 0LL
Tel: 01438 717000
http://www.cardinspirations.co.uk

The Craft Cottage
Unit 5a, Tonedale Business Park
Wellington
Somerset TA21 0AW
Tel: 01823 669055
Manufacturers and suppliers of a range of scoring boards.

Craftwork Cards
Units 6–8 Willow Court
Lotherton Way
Garforth
Leeds
LS25 2GB
Tel: 0113 7877794
http://www.craftworkcards.co.uk
Suppliers of cards and pre-scored cards in a range of colours and textures.

Creative Pastimes
Boulhurst Farm
Pains Hill
Limpsfield
Surrey RH8 0RG
Tel: 01883 730033
Suppliers of a huge range of craft materials.

Design Objectives
Unit 90, Woolsbridge Industrial Park
Three Legged Cross
Wimborne
Dorset BH21 6SU
Tel: 01202 811000
http://www.docrafts.co.uk
Distributors of a great range of tools and materials.

Kars & Co BV
PO Box 272
Aylesbury
Buckinghamshire HP18 9FH
Tel: 01844 238080
http://www.kars.nl
Manufacturers and distributors of a huge range of craft tools, materials and embellishments.

US and CANADA

American Art Clay Co, Inc
6060 Guion Road
Indianapolis, IN 46254-1222
Toll-free tel: 1-800-374-1600
http://www.amaco.com
Shop online for polymer clay, modelling tools and moulds.

Dover Publications
Customer Care Department
31 East 2nd Street
Mineola, NY 11501-3852
http://store.doverpublications.com
Shop online for books of stencils and art for cutting and pasting.

Great Impressions
Sierra Enterprises
PO Box 5325
Petaluma, CA 94955
Toll-free tel: 1-888-765-6051
http://www.sierra-enterprises.com
Shop online for rubber stamps, ink pads, embossing powders and heat guns.

Impress Rubber Stamps
120 Andover Park East
Tukwila, WA 98188
Tel: (206) 901-9101
http://www.impressrubberstamps.com
Shop in person or online for stamps and embellishments, including small metal charms.

The Japanese Paper Place
77 Brock Avenue
Toronto, ON M6K 2L3
Tel: (416) 538-9669
http://www.japanesepaperplace.com
Shop in person or online for speciality papers (some precut for cards) as well as art, calligraphy and printmaking supplies.

Keeping Memories Alive Scrapbooks.com
6624 East Main Street
Mesa, AZ 85205
Toll-free tel: 1-800-727-2726
http://www.scrapbooks.com
Shop online for papercraft supplies.

Loomis Art Store
254 St. Catherine Street East
Montreal, QC H2X 1L4
Toll-free tel: 1-800-363-0318
http://www.loomisartstore.com
Shop in person, by phone or visit the website for art and paper supplies. Stores located across Canada.

Loose Ends
2065 Madrona Avenue SE
Salem, OR 97302
Tel: (503) 390-7457
http://www.looseends.com
Shop in person or online for handmade and speciality papers, gift wrap and accessories.

Michaels
8000 Bent Branch Drive
Irving, TX 75063
Toll-free tel: 1-800-642-4235
http://www.michaels.com
/art/online/home
Visit the website or shop in person for craft supplies and speciality papers. Stores located across North America.

Scrapbook.com Superstore
116 North Lindsay Road No. 3
Mesa, AZ 85213
Toll-free tel: 1-800-727-2726
http://store.scrapbook.com
Shop online for papercraft supplies and accessories.

Acknowledgements

There are so many people I need to thank for their help on making this book that I really don't know where to begin. Thanks to my parents, Angel & Elvira, for all those years of support and constant teaching. Thanks to my sister Ananda, for being a great inspiration and my personal hero. Thanks to my husband, Omar, for being so supportive and understanding that dinner and cleaning could, and would, be done later.

Thanks to Marie for giving me the opportunity to write this book and believing in my ability to do it, and to Carly for helping me with the text and allowing her beautiful hands to be seen in the step-by-step pictures. Thanks to Elizabeth for her perfect design work and Colin, Michael and Sian for their great photography.

Thanks to Sarah Beaman for suggesting my name, Julie Hickey for all those wise words of advice and constant support, and last but not least, to Theresa and Faye Spreckley, the first two people to believe in my work and give me my dream job at Creative Pastimes.

And a big thank you to all those fellow crafters with whom I have enjoyed the joy of cardmaking and who have shared ideas and coffee with me: Martha, Pam, Wendy, Jane, Corinne, Kay, Carole, Lisa, Nicola, Katie, Jasmine, Hilda, Cass, Tracy, Sarah and Liz.